Vanishing Treasures

National Park Service
U.S. Department of the Interior

Vanishing Treasures Program

**Year End Report
Fiscal Year 2005 and
Proposed Activities for FY 2006**

May 2006

Contents

If you have any questions regarding the Vanishing Treasures Program, contact Virginia Salazar-Halfmoon (Virginia_Salazar-Halfmoon@nps.gov)

EXPERIENCE YOUR AMERICA

Acknowledgements

This report was edited Randy Skeirk and Jake Barrow, with assistance from Karen Fix, Jim Trott, and Glenn Simpson. Virginia Salazar-Halfmoon served as executive editor with Sande McDermott and Glen Fulfer providing guidance and review. Reports and photographs were provided by park VT staff unless otherwise noted. All FY1998-2004 data was taken from the 2004 VT report.

Front Cover: Skidoo Mill, Death Valley National Park. Cover photo by Glen Simpson. Cover design by Brett Seymour.

Executive Summary

This annual report, the eighth since the creation of the Vanishing Treasures Program, stands as a tribute to the Program's staff, Leadership Committee and Advisory Group. Over the years, they have developed and directed the Program, and ensured the continuation of it's extraordinarily successful cultural resource preservation efforts. Under their leadership, the Vanishing Treasures Program has proven to be the single most positive effort in preserving ancestral sites and historic architecture in the National Parks of the arid West.

Ten years ago, through a grass-roots initiative, park staff proposed and developed the Vanishing Treasures Program. Today, that Program continues to be the premiere source of ruins preservation work and training in the arid west National Parks.

This annual report highlights the individual accomplishments of Vanishing Treasures staff within their respective parks, as well as projects that parks have been able to execute with funding provided by the Vanishing Treasures Program.

Currently, the Vanishing Treasures Program provides preservation funding and staffing opportunities to 45 parks in Arizona, California, Colorado, Nevada, New Mexico, Texas, Utah and Wyoming. Park projects that receive funding are prioritized by the Advisory Group, which is composed of Vanishing Treasures personnel who work at the park level. The Leadership Committee, which directs and develops the priorities of the Program, is composed of superintendents from VT Parks.

In order to move the Vanishing Treasures Program into the future, modifications were made to improve the representation of participating parks on the Advisory Group and Leadership Committee and to provide greater flexibility in managing the Program. These changes were codified in 2005 when a committee of National Park Service staff developed the Program's first Charter.

This new Charter plots the direction of the Vanishing Treasures Program by clarifying the roles of the Leadership Committee and Advisory Group, and establishing the procedures the Program Coordinator will follow in supporting the Program in future years. One major change under the new Charter has the Program Coordinator reporting directly to the Intermountain Region's Deputy Associate Regional Director (DARD) for Cultural Resources. This will have the effect of elevating the profile of the Vanishing Treasures Program within the Directorate of the region. To facilitate communication with the DARD, the Program Coordinator's office has been moved to the Intermountain Region's Santa Fe Office.

Program support staff, including the Program's structural engineer and historical architect, continue to be duty-stationed in the parks, one at Mesa Verde National Park in Colorado and the other at Montezuma Castle and Tuzigoot National Monuments in central Arizona.

In order to ensure the broadest participation of park staff in Program leadership and advisory capacities, those participating in the drafting of the new VT Charter believed that a process needed to be established to designate terms, seek nominations either from the field or from park superintendents, and to elect representatives to the Leadership Committee and the Advisory Group on rotating terms.

As a result, the new VT Charter mandates a Leadership Committee with seven positions for superintendents who represent all of the parks within their designated states. These positions are identified as overlapping two-year or three-year appointments to ensure continuity as Committee members rotate out.

Under this new system, park superintendents from the Intermountain Region VT parks are eligible to nominate fellow superintendents to fill Leadership Committee positions. They then elect representatives from that pool of nominees. For the four VT parks located in the Pacific West Region, the process is different; the Desert Network simply submits their representative to the Leadership Committee. Following through on this new directive, the last three positions were recently filled, making the new Leadership Committee complete.

Similarly (with the exception of the representative from the Desert Network of the Pacific West Region) the six-member Advisory Group now has all new technical representatives.

This year, the list of parks requesting VT positions is not included in the Annual Report. The new Leadership Committee and Advisory Group is in the process of reviewing and modifying the old list based on newly developed criteria. This is an effort to ensure that positions are equitably distributed between those parks that have not previously received positions. This will ensure that parks in the Pacific West Region, who were not included in the Program at the time the original list was complied, will have the opportunity to request positions.

Finally, efforts are underway to develop a Vanishing Treasures website based in the Intermountain Region rather than in Washington, DC. This website will provide parks and partners access to current information and will serve as a central location to post training opportunities. A notice of the new web address will be sent out once the website is established.

Table 1.1. Vanishing Treasures Budget FY 1998-2005 (In Thousands of Dollars).

		VT Program Components			Total VT Program Expenditures	VT Park Base Increases		Total Base Increases	Total (Program plus Base)
		Projects	Training[2]	Management		Personnel	Additional		
FY 1998	Annual Budget	505.3	31.7	1	547	45		453	1,000
FY 1999	Annual Budget	123	8	3	164	58	237[1]	822	987
	Cumulative Total	628.3	40	44	712.3	1,038	237	1,275	1,987
FY 2000	Annual Budget	187	0	12	199	795		795	994
	Cumulative Total	815.3	71.7	56	910	1,833		2,070	2,981
FY 2001	Annual Budget	158	0	4	162	236		236	398
	Cumulative Total	973.3	71.7	60	1,072	2,069		2,306	3,379
FY 2002	Annual Budget	65	0	0	65	435		435	435
	Cumulative Total	1,038.3	71.7	60	1,137	2,504		2,741	3,814
FY 2003	Annual Budget	(7)	0	0	(7)	600		600	600
	Cumulative Total	1,031.3	71.7	60	1,130	3,104		3,341	4,414
FY 2004	Annual Budget	(33.6)	0	0	(33.6)	375		375	375
	Cumulative	997.7	71.7	60	1,096.4	3,479		3,716	4,789
FY 2005	Annual Budget	62.1	0	0	62.1	300		300	300
	Cumulative Total	1,059.8	70.3	60	1,158.5	3,779		4,016	5,089

Notes:

[1] $156.000 base increase for one park for personnel and an $81.000 park base increase.

[2] After 1998 training costs were added to the total cost for personnel and included in base increases

Message from the Vanishing Treasures Program Coordinator

It gives me great pleasure to introduce myself and the newly evolved Vanishing Treasures Program. My cultural heritage is deeply rooted in New Mexico; I am American Indian from Santa Clara Pueblo and Spanish, tracing this part of my ancestry back to the original colonizing families of New Mexico. My commitment to the preservation of cultural heritage and resources led me to a career with the National Park Service. During which time I held park assignments at Bandelier National Monument, Pecos National Historic Site, and White Sands National Monument. For a total of 16 years, of my 28 years, I served as the Regional Curator for the old Southwest Region through the transition to the Intermountain Region. Through this experience in a central office I gained the additional benefit of working with many parks and park staff; parks that are now members of the Vanishing Treasures Program. Visiting many of the VT parks provided insight into the challenges the parks have in the preservation of their cultural resource and the park's ability to obtain the needed assistance.

My continuing education, and the enhancement of my capabilities to better support the preservation of park cultural resources, includes this year spent as a participant of the USDA Graduate Program in the Executive Potential Program. This program broadened my leadership skills and provided the experience to view Vanishing Treasures programmatically, as an integral on-going preservation mechanism. The Executive Potential Program developed my ability to lead the VT program in identifying opportunities to expand the program's support base and to suggest ways to leverage funding to accomplish park preservation needs. My primary goal is to seek new paths to enable VT to continue as a viable, sustainable cultural preservation program. In addition, it is my personal challenge to help more people see their connection to the park resources, and to find ways the public can contribute that have not previously been utilized. I look forward to a year of expanded networking and cooperative efforts that will benefit both parks and partners. I am extremely excited to be a part of a team that will carry the

Vanishing Treasures Program into the future.

Virginia Salazar-Halfmoon

At-Large VT Staff

Preston Fisher
Structural Engineer, FY2000 Position
In continuing his longstanding tradition of providing structural engineering services to Vanishing Treasures parks, Preston assisted 11 park units either through site visits or telephone consultations. Preston's services included helping to plan the removal of an existing inappropriate concrete roof from Rooms 132 and 133 at Aztec Ruins National Monument, designing a more suitable lightweight roof, and providing Contracting Officer's Representative (COR) services for the project. In addition, he evaluated the structural stability and integrity of two old trading post buildings recently acquired by Aztec Ruins. At Fort Davis National Historic Site he reviewed plans and provided comments for stabilization treatments for the Post Commissary, while at the Mission San Juan Covento at San Antonio Missions National Historical Park he drafted a new slab design for a floor rehabilitation project.

In ongoing work, Preston compiled and analyzed structural engineering monitoring data for Pueblo Bonito at Chaco Culture Natural Historical Park, Square Tower and Cutthroat Tower at Hovenweep National Monument, and for structures at Wupatki National Monument. Also at Wupatki he recommended measures to mitigate damage caused by above average moisture incurred during the winter of 2004-2005.

At Tonto National Monument he reviewed plans and provided drawings for the construction of a retaining wall below the lower ruin, and at Natural Bridges National Monument he performed an initial structural assessment of site 42Sa6615 (NABR-14) near TeePee Ruin, and assisted the park Archeologist with emergency stabilization measures at that site.

Reaching across divisional boundaries, Preston assisted two Pacific West parks in California and Nevada. This included traveling to Mojave National Preserve to evaluate structural needs and options for

stabilizing and preserving the buildings associated with the Mineral Springs and Health Resort at Soda Springs, as well as evaluating the structural needs for several ranch structures at Valley View Ranch and for mine-related structures at the Evening Star Mine. Preston also provided assistance in the design and installation of a dive access platform at Devil's Hole in Death Valley National Park by way of a telephone consultation.

Duty stationed at Mesa Verde National Park, Preston serves all of that parks' VT engineering needs. In FY 2005 that included serving as COR for a contract to replace antiquated site shelter enclosure panels at Pit House "B", helping to develop the Structural Engineering module for the Archeological Site Conservation Program ArkDoc database, and contributing to the development of the stabilization module, developing field forms and instructions for recording the structural condition of sites, and mentoring two Fort Lewis College Interns.

Preston's mentoring duties included supervising the development and implementation of a structural component to the Archeological Site Conservation Program database for Mesa Verde National Park, and, during May, June, July, and August, overseeing the updating of existing information, the analysis and interpretation of monitoring data from structural monitoring points, and supplementing of geologic information for Site 5MV01406, known as Spring House. The interns also made several follow-up site visits to update structural engineering information from several other sites at the park.

In other park-related duties, Preston continued to monitor several of the park's prehistoric archeological sites, assisted in ranking several job applications at the park, and presented information to other park employees about structural engineering issues affecting archeological sites at training sessions for interpretative and backcountry rangers.

In general service to the Vanishing Treasures Program, Preston served on the

Vanishing Treasures SEPAS Panel in March and he completed *Baseline Standards and Guidelines for Conducting Structural Evaluations of Archeological Sites in the Field*, a document intended to assist anyone attempting to evaluate the structural stability of prehistoric structures.

In the Vanishing Treasures Program's tradition of interagency cooperation, Preston also assisted the Bureau of Land Management at two of their cultural resource sites. At Moon House in Southeastern Utah he produced a report outlining recommendations to stabilize and monitor a detached slab above the site, and at Canyon of the Ancients National Monument he evaluated stability concerns and made recommendations to help stabilize a damaged site. He also gave a talk – "Evaluating Prehistoric Sites" to the San Juan Basin Historical Society.

Randall Skeirik
Historical Architect, FY 2004 Position
New to both the National Park Service and to the southwestern United States, Randy joined the Vanishing Treasures team at the end of Fiscal Year 2004. As the Historical Architect for the Program, Randy is available to all 45 Vanishing Treasures parks to provide architectural and historic preservation consultation services on an as-needed basis. Over the course of 2005, he has focused his efforts on becoming acquainted with the wide array of Vanishing Treasures resources, their construction materials, and appropriate preservation techniques, and with other Vanishing Treasure staff.

Randy comes to the Program with over 15 years of experience as a historical architect working exclusively in the field of historic preservation; experience that runs the gamut from working with preservation architecture firms in the private sector, to nonprofit organizations including the Taliesin Preservation Commission, and two State Historic Preservation Offices.

At the request of the VT leadership, much of Randy's first year was focused on resources in Arizona, including Casa Grande Ruins National Monument, Organ Pipe Cactus National Monument, Grand Canyon and, of course, Montezuma Castle and Tuzigoot National Monuments, where he is stationed.

At Casa Grande, much effort is being directed at dealing with high populations of ground squirrels and pigeons, both of which are having detrimental effects on the historic resources. Working with Sande McDermott, Deputy Associate Regional Director for Cultural Resources, and Vanishing Treasures Program Manager, Virginia Salazar-Halfmoon, Randy helped to revamp a failed project proposal so that it specifically targeted needs at the site, and helped to find funding to address those needs. Work on this project will continue into FY 2006.

Randy also made several site visits to Organ Pipe to view and assess impacts on historic ranch sites in the park. Organ Pipe, located on the border with Mexico, is dealing with a number of difficult situations including damage from illegal immigrants and drug traffickers, Homeland Security impacts, and cross-border "raids" to steal building materials and fence posts from historic ranch buildings and corrals.

Randy has also conferred with Grand Canyon VT Archeologist Ellen Brennan on conservation and fire protection measures for such ephemeral wooden structures as the wikiups found on the North Rim.

At Montezuma Castle and Tuzigoot, in addition to his VT duties, Randy is acting as the Chief of the Resource Management Division. In that capacity, he is overseeing not only the work performed on Vanishing Treasures resources, but all of the park's cultural and natural resources. At Montezuma Castle and Tuzigoot a number of projects on VT resource were run concurrently, although none were funded with Vanishing Treasures project money.

These projects included the ongoing removal of inappropriate mortars from Tuzigoot; the documentation, mapping, and condition assessment of cavate sites at Montezuma Castle; and the assessment and development of treatment recommendations for Sinaguan masonry rooms at Montezuma Well.

Randy also participated in the development of the General Management Plan for Montezuma Castle and Tuzigoot, and helped establish the park's asset priority indices for use with the new Facility Management Software System (FMSS).

In March of 2005, Randy sat in on the Vanishing Treasures SEPAS Panel, and in

August participated in the historic
preservation field school held at the Post
Hospital at Fort Davis National Historical
Site. From Fort Davis, Randy went on to
Santa Fe to attend the first meeting of
the newly reconstituted VT Leadership
Committee.

Under the provisions of the new Vanishing
Treasures Charter, Randy sits as a
permanent, ex-officio member of the
Vanishing Treasures Advisory Group.

Training/Technical Assistance:
 During 2005, Randy completed training in
several different areas. He attended 80
hours of management training sessions, 40
hours each in Phoenix, Arizona and at
Glenn Canyon National Recreation Area. He
also became certified as a Contracting
Officer's Representative, and attended a
course outlining compliance documentation
requirements of the National Environmental
Policy Act (NEPA) and Section 106 of the
National Historic Preservation Act of
1966. In addition, he has completed NPS
Fundamentals I and is enrolled in
Fundamentals II early in 2006.

Vanishing Treasures Management Team

LEADERSHIP COMMITTEE
Chair, Lee Baiza, Superintendent Petrified
Forest NP
Corky Hays, Superintendent, Natural
Bridges and Hovenweep NM
Bruce Noble, Superintendent, Colorado NM
Curt Sauer, Superintendent, Joshua Tree NP
Todd Brindle, Superintendent, Fort Davis
NHS
Brad Traver, Superintendent, Tonto NM
Kayci Cook Collins, El Malpais and El
Morro NM

Program Management
Virginia Salazar-Halfmoon, VT **Program
Coordinator**
Randall Skeirik, VT Staff
Preston Fisher, VT Staff

ADVISORY GROUP
Angelyn Rivera, Bandelier NM
Jennifer Vavris, Canyon de Chelly NM
Robert Bryson, Mojave NP
Sarah Horton, Zion NP
Dave Evans, Chiricahua NM
Donald LaDeaux, Fort Laramie NH

Workshops and Training

Fort Davis Hospital Restoration

The Fort Davis National Historic Site Post Hospital Restoration kicked off with a three week historic preservation training workshop held at the site from July 18 through August 5, 2005. Restoration of portions of the hospital and the installation of new exhibits will provide Fort Davis and West Texas with a fascinating and educational window into 19th century medical practices. Participants included over forty individuals from Fort Davis, other units of the National Park Service, Cornerstones Community Partnerships, the Youth Conservation Corps, and the University of Vermont Graduate Program in Historic Preservation, as well as local volunteers, volunteers from other parts of the US, a preservation planner from Chattanooga, Tennessee, and volunteers from two other Universities.

The three week workshop was funded entirely by the Vanishing Treasures Program of the National Park Service and included instruction in historic plaster conservation, lime plastering, graffiti mitigation, 19th century window restoration, and floor reconstruction. It was a "hands-on" training opportunity that mixed students, outside experts, park service maintenance staff, and Vanishing Treasures personnel.

The park is the recipient of a Save America's Treasures Grant to assist with the project and the volunteer hours accumulated during this workshop provided over $30,000 in matching funds toward that grant. Based on the unqualified success of this workshop, a second preservation training workshop is being planned for the summer of 2006 which will be park funded.

2005 Workshop Participants

Sustainable Pest Management Workshop

A workshop focusing on sustainable management of vertebrate pests is planned for March of 2006. This workshop was funded in a large part from 2005 Vanishing Treasures funds. The purpose of this workshop/task force is to ensure that all appropriate voices are represented in our discussion of the problems and management issues related to Sustainable Pest Management (SPM) in Historic Resources (HR).

Included will be representatives of the following disciplines: natural resources; cultural resources; maintenance; and park management. The Resource Guides to be developed will provide Superintendents and other park managers with the information necessary so that the right questions may be asked of each of these voices when making decisions regarding SPM in HR. A task force will be established to see these Resource Guides through to completion.

The need for this type of guidance has been identified by the Associate Regional Directors for Natural and Cultural Resources, working under the direction of the Associate Director for Research and

Stabilization Forum – Bandelier

On November 9, 2005, a Stabilization Forum was hosted by Bandelier National Monument. The Stabilization Forum is an informal meeting of stabilization practitioners in VT parks which includes masons, exhibits specialists, archeologists, and architectural conservators. The purpose of these meetings (held 1-2 times yearly) is to share information on topics such as materials and methodology regarding fabric treatment of prehistoric masonry. Dialogue among the participants is facilitated by the host park, whose staff provides a site visit designed to promote further discussion.

At the 2005 meeting, 23 participants from Aztec Ruins National Monument, Bandelier National Monument, Chaco Culture National Historical Park, Fort Union National Monument, Pecos National Historical Park and Salinas Pueblo Missions National Monument were joined by the Superintendent of Jemez State Monument, as well as a Supervisory Exhibits Specialist from IMR-SF, and two representatives from the New Mexico State Historic Preservation Office. Participants discussed projects from the previous field season, looked at stabilization mortar test walls constructed at Bandelier, and visited the stabilized pueblos of Tyuonyi and Long House. Below is a summary of the topics discussed.

Stabilization Materials

Stewardship. There is a concern that, in addition to a lack of funding sources for programmatic solutions to interdisciplinary problems of this nature, solutions are often conceived and implemented either by maintenance personnel, or natural or cultural resource professionals with little or no cooperation with each other, or with park management. The development of these Resource Guides will be the first step toward correcting that deficiency.

The Vanishing Treasures Leadership Committee and the Vanishing Treasures Advisory Group are sponsoring and funding this workshop to address what has been identified as a long-standing problem that impacts their parks (as one Superintendent put it, "for forty years").

All of the participating parks use native or engineered soils, either unmodified or amended with various additives, to create earthen stabilization materials. The goal of selecting stabilization materials is to create a durable, natural-looking product (usually a replacement mortar) that is physically, visually and chemically compatible with the original masonry. Available soils differ widely in composition and appearance among the different parks, as do the masonry units and styles, deterioration conditions, and preservation challenges within the structures that are being treated; therefore, the choice of repair materials also varies among the parks.

Portland cement is a soil amendment used in mortar at Salinas Pueblo Missions, either alone or within proprietary stucco mixes. At Chaco, portland cement-amended earthen mortar is used in wall caps. An acrylic copolymer solution is added to earthen mortar at Jemez State Monument and Bandelier, and to plaster at Fort Union. Plaster at Salinas Pueblo Missions is modified with slaked ash. At Pecos, unmodified soil is used to make adobes. All of these materials reflect site managers' efforts to respond to the conservation needs of their sites, and are continually monitored and evaluated for their efficacy and appropriateness.

Treatment Methodologies

While masonry stabilization dominates the preservation activities at the parks, it is by no means the only type of conservation treatment. Backfilling of rooms or sites, also known as reburial, is an effective method of addressing preservation challenges. However, like all treatments, the materials must be compatible with original materials. At Aztec Ruins, one project is removing and replacing a previous backfilling treatment where the chosen materials had actually accelerated deterioration by promoting the movement of moisture and soluble salts through the walls. Backfilling is being used at Chaco, in rooms that are not accessible to the public, as a means of minimizing the impact of maintenance intervention on original masonry; this also reduces the volume of masonry that must receive cyclic maintenance.

Another way to reduce the effects of environmental deterioration on original materials is to divert weathering mechanisms such as rain, snow and wind to renewable repair materials. At Salinas Pueblo Missions, ash-amended soil plaster is used as a shelter coat on masonry buildings, and acrylic-amended soil covers adobe walls at Fort Union. These sacrificial layers also reduce the impact of cyclic maintenance on the masonry. At Pecos, adobes are used to encapsulate the original adobe walls of the mission, protecting them from weather and impacts from visitors and rodents.

Special Problems
In addition to correcting a previous backfilling treatment, Aztec Ruins staff removed an old concrete roof which sheltered a subterranean room. The treatment presented threats to the original architecture due to its design, including materials which contributed to its excessive weight, and poor construction. The removal of the roof was laborious and technically challenging, but the staff was able to accomplish it without damaging original wood and masonry elements.

At Pecos, burrowing pocket gophers destabilize wall foundations in the pueblo, causing uneven settling, displacing artifacts, and promoting erosion from severe rain events. Previous attempts to capture and relocate rodents have proven ineffective - the gophers simply return. This year, rodents were exterminated by directing motor vehicle exhaust fumes into their tunnels. The treatment is effective, and rodents are unlikely to reoccupy tunnels that contain gopher carcasses.

The meeting adjourned after the site visits, and Gary Brown of Aztec Ruins agreed to host next year's meeting.

Vanishing Treasures Parks in

Arizona

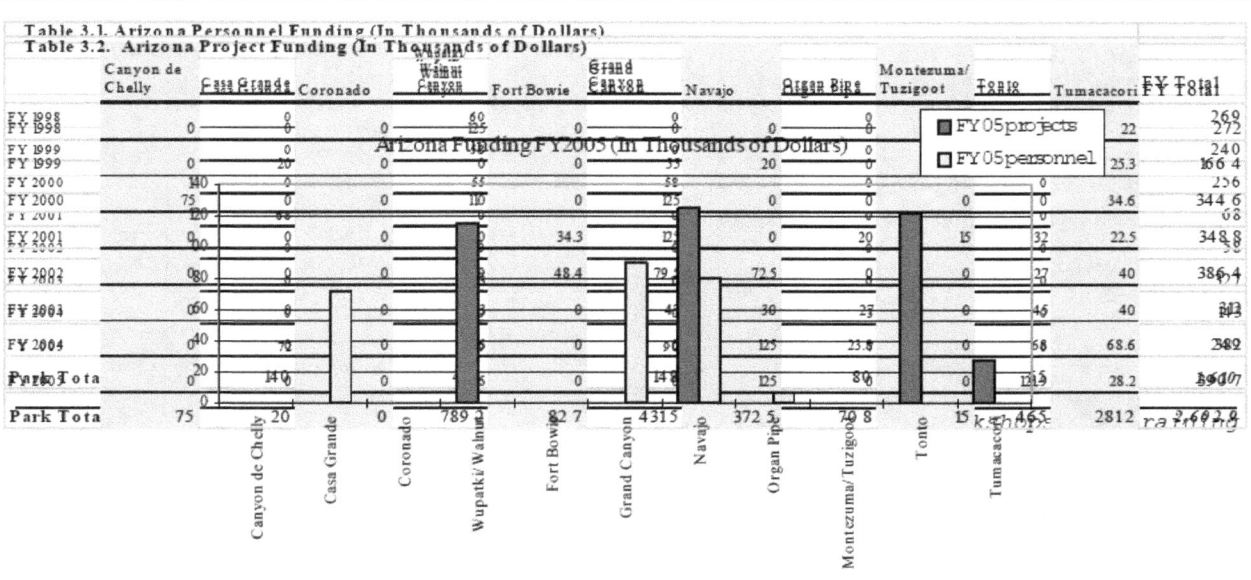

Table 3.1. Arizona Personnel Funding (In Thousands of Dollars)
Table 3.2. Arizona Project Funding (In Thousands of Dollars)

◆ Canyon de Chelly National Monument

Jennifer Lavris, Archeologist, FY 2002 Position

In FY 2005, Jennifer performed a variety of duties including program management, research, report writing and editing, project planning, database management, and various field projects. Office duties were primarily comprised of the day-to-day activities of co-managing the Canyon de Chelly archeology program, although she also monitored sites, managed archeological data, completed consultations, and assisted in general park planning efforts.

Jennifer served as co-project manager of the White House Ruin Documentation and Preservation Project and the Ruins Preservation of the Antelope House and Black Rock area. As an example of the leveraging of VT resources, both of these projects are being conducted through a cooperative agreement with Northern Arizona University. The White House Ruin Documentation and Preservation Project aims to collate existing White House Ruins data with 3D laser generated wall maps. This synthesized data will establish a baseline that will form the basis of future White House Ruins management recommendations. The laser scanning and planimetric mapping portions of this project have been sub-contracted to Western Mapping, Inc.

In another capacity, Jennifer has made substantial progress in an archival digital imaging project. These images will be used for future surveys and monitoring. The digitized images include historic photography and color slides and black & white prints from the 1990's Archeological Preservation Project. To date, over 6,400 total images have been digitized. Jennifer also continued to update and maintain the Canyon de Chelly ASMIS database, and in January she helped prepare a power point presentation on the topic of the Archeological Resource Protection Act given at the annual Canyon de Chelly Guides Training Workshop.

In the field, Jennifer assisted VT Archeologist Keith Lyons with several small-scale projects that included the survey of six kilometer-long parcels for the park-wide Watershed Restoration Project. These plots will be used to measure the impacts of exotic vegetation removal to the overall canyon system. Archeological surveys were necessary before any ground disturbance from exotic tree removal could occur. Jennifer and Keith also collaborated on the mapping of social roads and archeological sites along the South Rim road (NPS Route 10), from the canyon mouth to White House Overlook. This survey was conducted for an upcoming road re-surfacing project. In July, an inadvertent discovery of human remains required Jennifer and Keith to document and stabilize the site.

Training/ Technical Assistance provided:

In December 2004, Jennifer attended an Archeological Damage Assessment Class in Santa Fe, New Mexico. In January 2005, Jennifer attended the one-week NPS Fundamentals V training at the Mather Training Center located in Harpers Ferry, West Virginia.

In an example of inter-park cooperation, Jennifer spent 15 days on a Colorado River rafting trip assisting Grand Canyon VT Archeologist Ellen Brennan in conducting architectural documentation and condition assessments on several sites along the Grand Canyon River Corridor.

Keith Lyons, Archeologist, FY 2003 Position

In FY 2005, Keith performed a variety of duties including project management, site monitoring, research, report writing, project planning, collections and data management, archeological compliance and consultation, and various field projects. His office duties reflected the day-to-day activities of co-managing the Canyon de Chelly archeology program, while his research and writing tasks included devising the preliminary scope of work for Phase I of the Antelope House Site Management and Landscape Improvement Project, and creating scopes of work for Exotic Plant Removal at Ute Raid Pueblo.

Keith also developed the scope of work for Phase I survey, excavation, and investigation of the White House Ruin Site Management and Landscape Improvement Project, and then went on to oversee the project's implementation. This project is being conducted through a cooperative agreement with Northern Arizona University and was designed to remove unneeded erosion control features such as spider jetties and gabions from in front of the ruin, remove exotic vegetation from around the ruin and viewing area, and fence the ruin to enclose the previously unprotected artifact midden. The results of this phase of the work are improved safety conditions and enjoyment for visitors to the site, and the protection of sensitive archeological deposits. These improvements were accomplished in cooperation with the park's Maintenance Division and, through consultation with tribal members, was respectful of the sacred nature of the site. Keith is also overseeing the archival portion of this project which is now in the review stage.

In the field, Keith assisted VT archeologist Jennifer Lavris with several small-scale projects, including the survey of six kilometer-long parcels for the park-wide Watershed Restoration Project. These plots will be used to measure the impacts of exotic vegetation removal to the overall canyon system. Keith and Jennifer also collaborated on the mapping of social roads and archeological sites along the South Rim road (NPS Route 10), from the canyon mouth to White House Overlook. This survey was conducted for an upcoming road re-surfacing project. In July, an inadvertent discovery of human remains required Jennifer and Keith to document and stabilize the site.

Keith has also been given lead responsibility for Collections Management at the park which includes maintaining and updating the ANCS+ database. In January, Keith gave a power point presentation on the Archeological Resource Protection Act at the annual Canyon de Chelly Guides Training Workshop.

Training/ Technical Assistance provided:
In December 2004, Keith attended an Archeological Damage Assessment Class in Santa Fe, New Mexico. In January 2005, Keith attended the one-week NPS Fundamentals V training at the Mather Training Center located in Harpers Ferry, West Virginia.

In an example of inter-park cooperation, Keith spent 15 days on a Colorado River rafting trip assisting Grand Canyon VT Archeologist Ellen Brennan in conducting architectural documentation and condition assessments on several sites along the Grand Canyon River Corridor.

◆ Casa Grande Ruins National Monument

Rebecca Carr, Archeologist, FY 2005 Position
Casa Grande Ruins National Monument hired Rebecca in April of 2005. She holds a Bachelors degree from the University of Delaware with a double major in Anthropology and Art. She holds a certificate in museum curation at the undergraduate level and a Master of Science from the University of Pennsylvania Department of Historic Preservation.

Before working at Casa Grande, Rebecca worked at Mesa Verde National Park as Exhibit Specialist/Architectural Conservator and worked as an archeologist for URS Corp. and the University of Delaware Center for Archeological Research. Her work experience includes the Telluride Historical Museum, Anasazi Heritage Center, National Endowment for the Humanities, Bandelier National Monument and Mancos Historical Society.

Rebecca has worked with park staff, volunteers and contractors to compile previous documentation and treatment data into a usable digital format. This effort has led her to work with staff at WACC, SOAR, and the Santa Fe Regional Office. As a result, updated ASMIS records were submitted for all publicly accessible archeological sites. She also worked with Archeology Technician Nelda Creager to populate the research and treatment database with tabular survey data. Independent contractor, Greg Munson was hired to compile graphic data into a digital template for monitoring conditions within the Big House of Compound A.

At the beginning of this fiscal year, Rebecca attended GIS training with staff from Mesa Verde. This training proved useful in conducting staff needs assessments for a Southern Arizona parks GIS Plan. Further enhancement of the parks GIS capabilities were accomplished by incorporating highly detailed aerial photography into the GIS maps used for FMSS. These detailed aerial images will be of further use in the preservation planning for Compound A and Compound B.

In FY 2005, monitoring and assessment procedures were upgraded to quantify the impacts of animal damage to archeological resources. Rebecca participated in many discussions relating to Integrated Pest Management needs of this park. These discussions have resulted in a draft Environmental Assessment for the long term management and mitigation of animal impacts to vanishing treasures resources.

This emphasis on cultural resource planning led Rebecca to consult with Architects Randall Skeirik and Victoria Jacobson to gain insight into resource planning and more immediate NHPA compliance needs. It also led her to attend tribal meetings with representatives from the Ak-Chin Indian Community, Gila River Indian Community, Salt River Pima-Maricopa Indian Community, and the Tohono O'Odham Nation.

After coordinating with archeological staff at SOAR and at Tonto National Monument to standardize the data collection methods used at Casa Grande National Monument, Rebecca completed a preliminary condition survey of the walls of Compound A and Compound B to prioritize preservation needs. Rebecca has been working with Nalbert Chavez to methodically address each maintenance need that was identified in that survey.

Training/ Technical Assistance provided:
Rebecca attended GIS training, NEPA and NHPA Compliance training, attended the Third Annual Arizona Statewide Historic Preservation Partnership Conference, and attended a one day workshop on earthen construction methods where she learned to prepare rammed earth soil testing samples and gained hands-on experience constructing a rammed earth building.

Nalbert Chavez, Masonry Worker, FY 2005 Position
Nalbert Chavez was converted to a Vanishing Treasures position in 2005. Nalbert has worked for Casa Grande Ruins National Monument for 37 years. A primary duty of his position has been treatment and maintenance of the exposed architecture in Compound A and Compound B. His practical knowledge of preservation materials has been gained through hands-on preservation. This year, the Vanishing Treasures program concentrated on documenting existing resources as a precursor to preservation treatments. His knowledge of previous

work and practical treatment practices has been of considerable benefit to the success of this program in 2005.

With assistance from the Vanishing Treasures maintenance staff and a contracted photographer, all of the drains within Compound A were photographed, mapped and made functional once again. Twenty-three walls within Compound A and all exposed architecture within Compound B were photographically documented. Maintenance treatments were completed for twelve walls within Compound A and the improved monitoring plan was implemented to quantify animal damage.

Rebecca Carr surveying Compound B walls

Use of Lapse Funds:
In FY 2005, lapsed salary was used to fund the previous Exhibit Specialist position to hire, train and supervise Vanishing Treasures staff. It was also used to purchase supplies and equipment needed to fulfill the preservation needs of Casa Grande Ruins National Monument. Supplies were purchased for the documentation and condition monitoring of this park's cultural resources. Examples of supplies and equipment purchased in support of VT work are: a field computer, computer program upgrade to AutoCAD 2006, a GPS unit, measuring tapes, camera tripod, photo scale and basic documentation materials. Materials needed for preservation treatment were also purchased this year. Examples include treatment soil, ceramic microspheres, glass microtags, soil analysis equipment, and soil additives.

In FY 2005, a maintenance storage building was identified for reallocation of use. Its new use in FY 2006 will be a workshop for the Vanishing Treasures program. This workshop will be set up for soils analysis and treatment testing. While this workshop will be in daily use by the Vanishing Treasures employees of Casa Grande Ruins National Monument, this facility may also serve as a resource for other VT parks within the SOAR network. Thus, the use of lapsed salary for supplies and equipment in 2005 will enhance our ability to efficiently maintain and preserve cultural resources in the future.

◆ Grand Canyon National Park

Ellen Brennan, Archeologist, FY 2000 Position
During FY 2005, with the use of lapse funds, Ellen implemented preservation treatments at the Tusayan and Walhalla Glades Pueblos. Phil Wilson and Marc LeFrancois from Salinas Pueblo Missions NM provided guidance with the planning and implementation of those projects. Keith Lyons and Jennifer Lavris, of Canyon de Chelly NM assisted Ellen on a Colorado River Fund river trip. The group recorded the architectural condition of 30 masonry features in the Deer Creek drainage as part of Ellen's continued work in that area. Keith, Jennifer, and Ellen completed Level I architectural documentation of sites in the Stone Creek drainage, monitored the condition of VT eligible sites along the river corridor, and performed limited preservation maintenance at the Boucher Cabin site during the river trip.

Ellen oversaw the fire archeology program for most of the summer. She also assisted with day-to-day archeology program activities. Ellen continued to manage the lab and the branch Volunteer-in-Park program. Ellen continues as a member of the park's ARPA taskforce. Ellen planned and supervised the Hermit Road cultural resource inventory project in advance of the road improvement/greenway project under consideration for that area. Ellen serves on the interdisciplinary planning team for the Hermit Road project and she supervised and trained a Grand Canyon Park Foundation intern in ruins preservation activities this past summer. Ellen wrote the compliance packages for the preservation projects implemented in FY 2005 and developed the proposals for VT funding in PMIS. She developed and

implemented Arizona Archeology Day activities with interpreter Ilyse Goldman. These activities took place at the Tusayan Ruin and Museum in March 2005. Finally, Ellen presented talks on Grand Canyon archeology to guides working for the Grand Canyon Field Institute.

Training/ Technical Assistance provided:
Ellen assisted with ruins preservation activities at Wupatki National Monument for one week this past summer, receiving valuable hands-on experience in masonry work from Lloyd Masayumptewa, Lyle Balenquah, and Ian Hough. Ellen participated as a speaker at the Arizona State Historic Preservation Conference, Tucson, Arizona. Her presentation focused on the link between NPS Management Policies and the Vanishing Treasures program.

Tusayan Kiva A

Use of Lapse Funds:
Ian Hough was hired under the Vanishing Treasures base increase at Grand Canyon National Park near the end of fiscal year 2005. However, Ian's EOD date fell in fiscal year 2006 (October 3, 2005).

Ellen Brennan used lapse funds for a number of Vanishing Treasures projects and program improvements. These included: the purchase of a computer for the new VT archeologist; purchase of upgraded data collection and drafting equipment and software packages; purchase of stabilization materials and supplies for the implementation of preservation projects at the Walhalla Glades and Tusayan Pueblo sites; personnel services costs for Grand Canyon permanent, term, and seasonal employees assisting with the implementation of the preservation projects; travel expenses for two employees from Salinas Pueblo Missions to provide guidance for the Tusayan and Walhalla preservation projects; rental fees for the use of GSA summer seasonal vehicles to support the VT program and project activities; and the award of a contract to upgrade the Vanishing Treasures database (architectural documentation data) and integrate it with the Grand Canyon Site, ASMIS, and photographic databases.

◆ Montezuma Castle National Monument and Tuzigoot National Monument

Alex Contreras, Masonry Worker, FY 1999 Position
Throughout 2005, Alex continued to build on his work at Tuzigoot with the help of Stefan Sloper, a returning mason from the 2004 field season. As in previous years, the ruins stabilization at Tuzigoot was guided by ongoing research and documentation conducted by our archeological team lead by John Schroeder (VT archeologist) and 4 STEP archeologists; Travis Ellison, Maggie Bowler, Jeremy Omvig, and Jacki Mullen. Using documentary research and field survey, they are documenting and recording the various phases of repair and reconstruction at Tuzigoot. Through these efforts the Park is now able to determine which areas contain inappropriate mortar types, and direct the efforts of the masonry team to those sections of the ruin that are most imperiled by hard modern portland cement mortars.

In addition to the replacement of inappropriate pointing mortars with a softer soil cement/mortar mix, Alex has continued removing 1960's era wall capping. This capping, which also utilized portland cement, incorporated projecting stonework that was intended to discourage visitors from walking or sitting on the walls. The jagged appearance of the projecting stones contrasted sharply with the prehistoric stonework and interfered with the visitor's appreciation of the site. The 1960's capping also encouraged the retention of moisture inside the wall, and accelerated the deterioration of the remaining prehistoric mortar, so the result of the recapping effort is both

aesthetic and functional. The new wall caps create a consistent and unified appearance to the ruin that enhances the visitors' experience while providing a more porous mortar that will prevent the accelerated deterioration of the remaining prehistoric mortar and stone.

Over the course of the year, Alex replaced 879 linear ft. of capping, completed 340 sq. ft. of repointing and 108 linear ft. of basal repair. Seventy eight sq. ft. of deteriorated stone was also replaced.

John Schroeder, Archeologist, FY 1999 Position (Converted in 2004)
John began work at Tuzigoot in February 2003 as a STEP archeologist conducting condition assessments and documentation. In 2005, after a VT funded masonry position was vacated, it was converted to that of an archeologist and John was moved into the position as a SCEP. Since that time John has assumed the responsibilities of park archeologist, overseeing work at several sites in Montezuma Castle, Montezuma Well and at Tuzigoot.

Acting Chief Ranger Karen Hughes escorting an archeological assessment team up to Montezuma Castle.

Prior to his employment with the National Park Service, John completed a Bachelor of Arts degree in anthropology at the University of California, Los Angeles, and has worked as an archeologist in California, Utah, Colorado, and the north coast of Peru. He is currently finishing up his Master's degree at Northern Arizona University.

In his role as park archeologist, John started two new condition assessment and documentation projects this year in addition to continuing the work at Tuzigoot. In addition, John has assumed collateral duties including compliance coordinator, collections manager, and research coordinator. John is working closely with the park's affiliated tribal groups to encourage greater cooperation among the various organizations.

Training/ Technical Assistance provided:
In 2005 John completed NEPA/Section 106 training sponsored by the National Park Service and held at Bryce Canyon. In December of 2004 he attended an ARPA damage assessment class conducted by Archeological Research Investigations at the National Park Service's Santa Fe office. John also attended the 2005 Society of American Archeology meetings in Salt Lake City, Utah.

♦ **Navajo National Monument**

Brian Culpepper, Archeologist, FY 2000 Position
In FY 2005 Brian continued overseeing the day-to-day operations and program management of Navajo's Cultural Resource Division, a position he has held since July 2003. He devoted much of his energy to the planning, coordination, and direction of the architectural documentation and condition assessment project for Keet Seel. He also continued duties as the monument's Section 106/NEPA compliance coordinator, served as the monument's GPRA coordinator, and organized and supervised preservation treatment at Keet Seel. Additionally he continued duities as the administrator for the Planning, Environment, and Public Comment (PEPC) electronic compliance tracking system, the Research Permit and Reporting System (RPRS) coordinator, and collateral duty as the monument's collection manager. During the fiscal year Brian attended supervisor training, a cultural awareness seminar, the NPS S270 basic air operations and S271

helicopter crewmember course, and a contracting officer's technical representative refresher course.

Kenny Acord, Archeological Technician/ Archeologist, FY 1998 Position
Kenny was hired in January of 2004 under the Student Career Experience Program (SCEP). He worked full-time for much of the year, but switched to part-time schedule in order to finish his thesis research. He defended his thesis in May, successfully completing the requirements for a Master's of Arts in Anthropology from Northern Arizona University. In September he was converted to permanent full-time as a GS-0193 Archeologist. During the fiscal year Kenny continued with the time-consuming work on researching and documenting the history of archeological research and preservation treatment activities at Keet Seel as part of the architectural documentation and condition assessment project. Culled from numerous and often incomplete and ambiguous source information, Kenny's research will form the historical and photographic baseline information used to record the architectural features and rooms in future fieldwork. Kenny also participated in preservation treatment at Keet Seel, and completed the NPS S270 basic air operations and S271 helicopter crewmember course.

Vacant, Archeological Technician, FY 2005

Use of Lapse Funds:
The bulk of lapse funding was used to purchase field and office equipment/supplies; and software in direct support of the monument's VT program, particularly for the Keet Seel architectural documentation project. Portions were used to extend a contract with the Museum of Northern Arizona to inventory and re-house NAVA objects and archives in their collections and for a personal services contract with Fred Blackburn to conduct background research of Keet Seel. The remaining funds were used for travel/training costs incurred during the year.

Project Completion Reports
Architectural Documentation and Condition Assessment of Keet Seel Cliff Pueblo - $125,000
In 2005, the Vanishing Treasures Initiative provided Navajo National Monument with funding to continue the

LIDAR mapping phase of the Keet Seel architectural documentation and condition assessment project that commenced in FY2004. As in the previous fiscal year, fieldwork was conducted under a cooperative agreement with Northern Arizona University and the Colorado Plateau Cooperative Ecosystem Studies Unit, utilizing the services of subcontractor Western Mapping Company. Fieldwork consisted of establishing geodetic control and aerial photography/photogrammetric topography of the Keet Seel and Betatakin units.

Permanent geodetic control points in the area of Keet Seel and Betatakin cliff pueblos were established to facilitate the referencing of future mapping data to a standardized geodetic reference coordinate system (UTM) and horizontal (NAD83/WGS84) and vertical (NAVD88) datums. This effort enables the use of LIDAR mapping data of Keet Seel, and any future mapping data of other sites, in a unified GIS environment and other file formats. Color stereo aerial photography was collected at a 1:6800 scale and the photogrammetrically-produced topography was produced at a 1.0 meter contour interval, making planimetric maps available for all modern physiography within both environments.

◆ Tonto National Monument

Duane C. Hubbard, Cultural Resources Program Manager (Archeologist), FY 2000 Position
During FY05, Duane supervised a variety of cultural resource projects including condition assessments at three of the five primary cliff dwellings in the Monument. Intensive condition assessments included completing condition data sheets and annotating impacts on photographs for 231 individual wall faces. Duane also conducted monitoring and condition assessment for over half of the Monument's 63 sites. Many of the sites had condition information that was nearly 20 years old. Duane continued establishing relationships with numerous Native American Tribes and the Arizona State Historic Preservation Office.

Duane continued working with WACC and the University of Arizona on an extensive photographic backlog project focused on historic photographs of the sites in the Monument as well as past ruins preservation activities. Duane also continued a stabilization history project with the Northern Arizona University Anthropology Department and worked closely with the Archeological Research Institute at Arizona State University to analyze and catalog artifacts collected during ruins preservation projects. Duane continues to manage the park's Archeological Sites Management Information System (ASMIS), Automated National Catalog System (ANCS), Planning, Environment and Public Comment (PEPC) and established park cultural resource databases for photographs, site monitoring and condition assessment. Duane participated as a SEPAS panel member for the Vanishing Treasures Program and participated as a member of Vanishing Treasures Charter Team which finalized the program charter in 2005. In addition to Duane's VT responsibilities, he was involved in archeological research, curation, consultation and compliance.

Project Completion Reports
Preservation Documentation/Treatment of Three Primary Cliff Dwellings at Tonto National Monument – $121,900
Tonto received funding in FY05 for the first year of a documentation and treatment project for three prehistoric cliff dwellings (TONT 50 - eight rooms outside the dripline, TONT85A-39, TONT85A-44). The project has two phases: (Phase I, FY05) perform baseline documentation for the creation of 3D geo-referenced, metrically accurate, high-resolution laser scan for all three sites; (Phase II, FY06) equalize differential fill loads, improve on-site drainage, replace eroded mortar through capping and repointing, and mitigate cracks in prehistoric adobe plaster.

Field condition assessments, database construction, background research and reporting were undertaken by Duane Hubbard (TONT Archeologist), Matt Guebard (TONT Archeological Technician) and Jeanne Stevens Schofer (Northern Arizona University Archeologist). The team spent most of the summer season performing condition assessments at the three cliff dwellings. Intensive condition assessments included completing condition data sheets and annotating impacts on photographs for 231 individual wall faces. Despite numerous bear and rattlesnake encounters, swarms of Africanized bees and heat in excess of

110 degrees, all field and lab work was accomplished on schedule.

High quality graphics documentation including laser scanning models and survey were completed by 4-G Consulting and Western Mapping Company. The surveying project established accurate UTM coordinates and sea level elevation for permanent datums near the Upper Cliff Dwelling and two smaller ruins (TONT85A-39, TONT85A-44). This control will be used for current and future mapping, monitoring, and pretreatment documentation. Surveying the location of all existing and identifiable datums used by previous researchers conducting excavations or other investigations at or near these three sites was included in this project.

High-resolution 3D scanning of TONT85A-39, TONT85A-44 and the caves in which they are located was also accomplished. All scanning was geo-referenced and the data produced from this effort was integrated into the monument's GIS. Scanning resolution varied from 2 cm scan resolution for the cave exteriors to 2 mm for cave interior, features, and architecture. The scanned data was used to produce 3D TIN models for use in the development of planimetric maps and architectural sheets for both sites. Finally, the contractors acquired 5MP digital color photography of all site architecture which depicts each wall face and wall top in a series of overlapping photographs. This photography enables the production of scaled architectural sheets of all wall faces and the production of a professional quality animation of each ruin and the local environment.

Arizona State University and the Western Archeological Conservation Center were also contracted to assist in artifact analysis, historic photography research and cataloging of artifacts collected during the course of this project.

The objectives identified for this fiscal year were accomplished in full. All pretreatment, condition assessment, and architectural baseline information was accomplished for TONT 39. TONT 44. A formal condition assessment was collected for TONT 50. Once Phase II is completed in FY06, the results of the project will produce an increase in the condition of the resources from fair to good (TONT 50)

and from poor to good (TONT 39, 44) as defined by LCS condition definitions.

During the fiscal year, one draft completion report was prepared and one professional paper was presented at the Third Annual Arizona Statewide Historic Preservation Partnership Conference, June 8-11, 2005, Tucson, Arizona.

Budget
One archeological technician (student appointment) was hired at the Monument to assist in field documentation and lab work (7% of allocation). Approximately 5% of the project money was used to buy supplies to support the project effort, 3% was used for equipment, and 1% was used for travel in support of the project. The remaining 85% of the funds were allocated to pretreatment documentation contracts with the Northern Arizona University Anthropology Department, Arizona State University, The Western Archeological Conservation Center, and 4-G Consulting and Western Mapping Company.

◆ Tumacacori National Historic Park

Jeremy Moss, Archeologist, FY 2000 Position
In FY 05 Jeremy continued working with WACC on the cultural inventory of the newly acquired lands. Excavation focused on the mission orchard wall and the room block that extends 200 yards to the south of the church. Jeremy is also completing lithic analysis and soil descriptions for the final report.

Over the past year most of Jeremy's time has been spent on a preservation history documenting the last 90 years of preservation work at San Jose de Tumacacori. This report documents past preservation efforts using historic photos, photos from reports, and summaries of past projects. The report is essentially a room by room and wall by wall history of preservation. One of the goals of the project is to create a database of all preservation treatments and interventions completed on the mission church and associated ruins. Two documents will be printed, one intended for use by interpretive staff, the other for use by preservation/maintenance staff. The reports will be completed by December and will benefit preservation/maintenance staff and interpretation.

Last summer Jeremy worked for three weeks with the FLAG preservation crew on repointing and capping at Wupatki NM, as part of his training program. Jeremy is also designing a plaster research project with the goal of identifying the limestone source from which lime plaster was processed. Jeremy continues to provide assistance with compliance issues as they arise.

David Yubeta, Exhibits Specialist, FY 1998 Position

David served as project manager for VT projects at Tumacacori's three mission sites. He also served in this capacity for six VT preservation projects at JOTR and MOJA. David participated in projects at Mills Canyon, New Mexico, providing expertise in preservation intervention to students from Snow College and the Cibola National Forest. He also participated as project leader for the Forest Service at Sabino Canyon in stabilization of the 12 CCC era bridges. David served as point of contact for training sessions held at Tumacacori for NPS facility managers and for Forest Service archeologists, instructing on lime plaster stabilization techniques at Brown Canyon Ranch. David participated in condition assessments at SAGU parks historic CCC era picnic areas. David continues to provide a three day workshop on earthen architecture to students in the Traditional Building Skills curriculum at Snow College, Ephraim, Utah.

Ray Madril, Masonry Worker, FY 1998 Position

During FY 2005, Ray participated in various projects throughout the southwest. Ray assisted the BLM, San Pedro District, in capping the ruin walls of Terranate in nearby Fairbank, Arizona. Ray also assisted preservation specialists and stone masons at MOCA in a joint park project. Ray was called in to provide emergency stabilization at JOTR on the walls of Ryan Ranch which had been heavily impacted from winter rains. He participated in lime plastering those walls later in the year. Ray also assisted in stone masonry repairs at Wupatki Visitor Center rebuilding and replacing historic stone elements. Ray was involved in the preservation of Mills Orchard Ranch located in New Mexico, rebuilding and replacing stone and lime plaster on a late 1880s ranch house and

associated outbuildings. This Forest Service project lasted for five weeks. He once again participated in repair of the historic CCC bridges at Sabino Canyon for the Forest Service. Ramon also participated in stabilization efforts at Cary's Castle, a wilderness site located in JOTR. Late in the fiscal year, Ramon finished the preservation year by stabilizing the ruins of Fort Piute located at MOJA and carrying out emergency stabilization at Keys Ranch at JOTR.

Ray worked on stabilization efforts on the bell tower of the Franciscan church at Tumacacori, repointing the fired brick and in-filling voids. Ray also participated in condition assessments at SAGU on the CCC era picnic areas. Additionally, Ray helped out in providing logistical and technical assistance at Brown Canyon Ranch House in southeast Arizona, for the Forest Service, instructing FS personnel on preservation techniques regarding lime plaster application. Ray also assisted in providing logistical assistance for the facility manager's cultural resource training session hosted by Tumacacori NHP.

Repointing Bell Tower at Tumacacori

Project Completion Reports
Repointing of Historic Bell Tower - $28,200

FY 2005 funding was utilized to re-point and replace loose and missing brick on the park's historic mission bell tower. Approximately 95% of the funding was to provide personnel services for this labor intensive project. Scaffolding was erected on the interior of the bell tower and preservation staff re-pointed fired adobe brick mortar joints and infilled voids with lime plaster and fired adobe brick cobbling. The new plaster was patinized with soil-tinted water to subdue the natural white color and more closely match the original fired adobe.

♦ Wupatki National Monument and Walnut Canyon National Monument

Al Remley, Archeologist, FY 1998 Position
In FY 2005, Al performed a variety of duties including research report writing and editing, database maintenance, technical support, numerous field projects and VT Program support. Office duties were primarily comprised of the day-to-day activities of managing the Flagstaff Areas Archeology Program including budget formulation, project and personnel supervision, and performance management.

Specific program accomplishments include preparing the FLAG Areas ASMIS Corrective Action Plan, writing 15 SEPAS project proposals, and completing the Secretary of Interior's Report, the various required year end reports for SEPAS funded projects, and the annual VT accomplishment reports. In combination with the Intermountain Region's Core Operations evaluation process, Al participated in formulating the FLAG area Park's Business Plan, and he assisted the former VT Program Coordinator in completing the FY04 Year End Report by editing and formatting the publication and supervising its printing.

Finally, at the Arizona Historical Society Conference in Tucson last June, Al presented a paper focused on the need for developing sustainable preservation programs based upon realistic needs and evaluations of historic structures and how they will be used, interpreted, and preserved. This paper was co-authored by Todd Metzger and Lloyd Masayumptewa.

Walnut Canyon
Throughout FY2005, Al continued to work with the Department of Anthropology at Northern Arizona University to continue mapping First Fort at Walnut Canyon. This was a VT project funded in FY04 and is continuing as a working project through FY06 through a cooperative agreement with the Colorado Plateau Cooperative Ecosystems Study Unit. Al also prepared a second cooperative agreement with Northern Arizona University that included an archeological testing plan and research design for testing two small sites at Walnut Canyon.

Wupatki
At Wupatki, two significant VT related projects were conducted in FY05. The first involved completion of the documentation and treatment of Crack-In-Rock and Middle Mesa Pueblos, two sites that are situated alongside each other in Wupatki's backcountry. This project was partially funded in FY04 and then fully funded in FY05. Both sites were documented and several structures received minor stabilization treatments to maintain them in good condition.

In the front country, the winter of 2004-2005 proved especially damaging to Wupatki Pueblo. Extensive snow and the resulting melt-off caused moisture, freeze thaw, and exfoliation damage to numerous rooms at Wupatki. After consulting with Preston Fisher, VT's Structural Engineer, emergency stabilization was completed in June. The project was made into a training opportunity and folks from GRCA, NAVA, MOCA, and TUMI came to Wupatki to help complete this emergency work. The Flagstaff Area Park staff could not have completed this important stabilization project without this extra help and thanks go out to all the parks that shared their personnel and expertise.

Finally, work on the WUPA/SUCR entrance road has required Al's input on the Environmental Assessment. The project will involve repaving 13+ miles of road and reconfiguring some front country parking lots, and will require the development of archeological testing/data recovery plans. Sue Wells at WACC has been especially helpful in providing examples of data recovery plans and compliance letters to SHPO and the Advisory Council.

Ian Hough, Archeologist, FY 2003 Position
Throughout the fall of 2004 and spring of 2005, Ian continued preservation documentation and treatment work at Middle Mesa Pueblo at Wupatki National Monument. Over the summer, he went on to prepare the final report of the preservation work that was conducted for this project. In addition, Ian assisted with emergency preservation treatment at

Wupatki Pueblo and he continued overseeing the park-wide archeological site condition monitoring program, which includes the collection of architectural condition assessment information at Wupatki and Walnut Canyon National Monuments.

Also during 2005, Ian prepared numerous SEPAS funding proposals for ruins preservation projects to be conducted between 2005 and 2010 at Wupatki and Walnut Canyon National Monuments. He worked with VT Structural Engineer Preston Fisher and FLAG Areas preservation specialists to conduct emergency condition assessments of rooms affected by above-average precipitation at Wupatki Pueblo over the winter of 2004/2005.

Finally, Ian coordinated FLAG Areas events for the 2005 Flagstaff Festival of Science, including an open house that featured ruins preservation in National Park Service archeology.

Training/ Technical Assistance provided:
In April 2005, Ian completed hearing testing and First Aid/CPR training.

Lyle J. Balenquah, Archeologist, FY 2000 Position
In 2005, Lyle served as the project work leader for numerous projects at Wupatki National Monument and was involved in numerous assignments related to the Vanishing Treasures Program. Lyle's office duties included producing compliance packets and writing project completion reports for 2005 preservation projects at Wupatki National Monument. In addition, Lyle wrote and submitted SEPAS project proposals to be conducted through the year 2010.

Lyle's field projects this year included leading an emergency repair project at Wupatki Pueblo that included a consultation with Preston Fisher, Vanishing Treasures Structural Engineer; preparing the compliance documents; assembling a crew from multiple parks including the Grand Canyon, Navajo National Monument, Montezuma Castle, and Tumacacori; supervising the fieldwork; and writing the completion report. In addition, Lyle, along with Ian Hough, completed the Crack-In-Rock and Middle Mesa VT stabilization and documentation project.

In July, Lyle, along with Lloyd Masayumptewa and Woody Coochwytewa (NPS Archeological Technician), assisted Navajo National Monument Archeologist, Brian Culpepper, in training their preservation crew in stabilization techniques. Training occurred on site at Kawestima (Keet Seel).

Finally, Lyle assisted in preparing the FY 2004 Vanishing Treasures Year End Report by compiling all the projects funded by Vanishing Treasures in that year. This included editing submittals, formatting chapters, and compiling photos submitted from parks.

Training/ Technical Assistance provided:
Training this year has been limited to telnet courses that included the following: "Personal Safety and Security What Every Employee Should Know" Finished Aug 02, 2005, "Heat Injury Prevention: Cool Ideas On A Hot Topic (AM session)" Finished Apr 19, 2005, "Introduction to PEPC (Planning, Environment, and Public Comment)" Finished Apr 13, 2005. He also participated in an online ladder safety training in May.

Vanishing Treasures Parks in
California/Nevada

<u>Pacific West Region Orientation Trip</u>
In 2001 the Pacific West Region became members of the Vanishing Treasures Program.

In early October 2005 an orientation trip was made by the Deputy Regional Director of Pacific West Region, Cicely Muldoon, PWR Chief of Cultural Resources, Stephanie Toothman, Joshua Tree Superintendent, Curt Sauer, Intermountain Region Deputy Associate Regional Director, Sande McDermott and the VT Program Coordinator, Virginia Salazar-Halfmoon.

The trip served to provide awareness of the Vanishing Treasures Program to superintendents and resource staffs of Death Valley National Park, Manzanar National Historic Site and Joshua Tree National Park. Each of the parks has identified Vanishing Treasures resources. Time prohibited a visit to Mojave National Preserve, another of the Pacific West Region Vanishing Treasures Program parks. The Team discussed opportunities for potential future projects and learned about the network system in place for sharing resources and staff among the Desert Network parks. Park staff provided the Team with tours to sites preserved through the use of Vanishing Treasures funds.

The change in Pacific West representation to the Leadership Committee, from the Superintendent of Mohave National Preserve to the Superintendent of

Today, Manzanar has been established as a separate site. The Vanishing Treasures Program acknowledges the cultural resources the park is preserving.

Joshua Tree National Park, determined the need and timing of the orientation trip. In addition, the Team met with the new Superintendent of Manzanar National Historic Site to evaluate Vanishing Treasures resources and to discuss the recognition of Manzanar as an independent unit of the Vanishing Treasures Program.

Pacific West Region is very receptive to the Vanishing Treasures Program and looks forward to their continued involvement in the program.

California

ojects & Personnel Accomplishments

Manzanar was previously a unit managed by Death Valley National Park.

Vanishing Treasures Parks in
Colorado

Table 3.3. Colorado Personnel Funding (In Thousands of Dollars)

	Dinosaur	Mesa Verde	FY Total
FY 1998	0	67	67
FY 1999	0	4	4
FY 2000	0	261	261
FY 2001	0	0	0
FY 2002	0	0	0
FY 2003	0	0	0
FY 2004	0	162	162
FY 2005	0	0	0
Park Total	0	494	*494*

Table 3.4. Colorado Project Funding (In Thousands of Dollars)

	Dinosaur	Mesa Verde	FY Total
FY 1998	0	67	67
FY 1999	0	4	4
FY 2000	0	261	261
FY 2001	0	0	0
FY 2002	0	0	0
FY 2003	0	0	0
FY 2004	0	162	162
FY 2005	0	123.9	123.9
Park Total	0	617.9	*617.9*

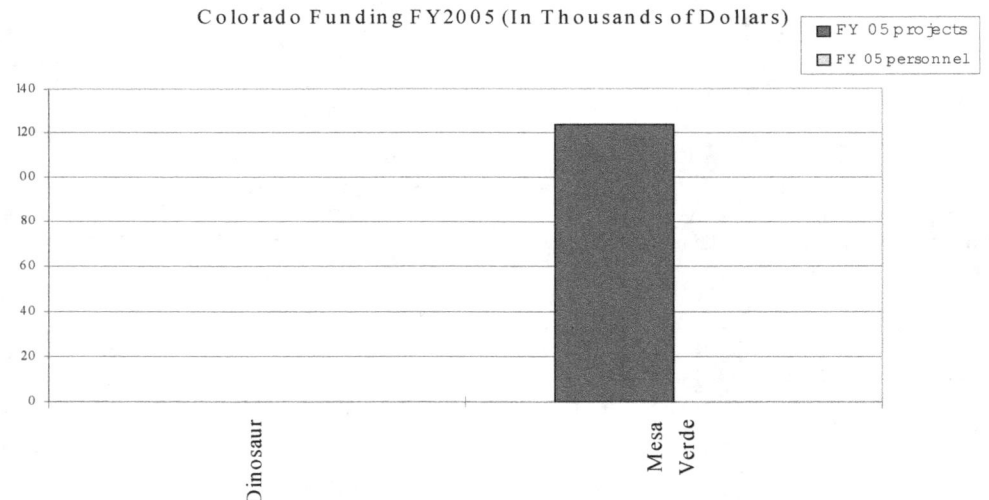

Colorado Funding FY2005 (In Thousands of Dollars)

- FY 05 projects
- FY 05 personnel

Mesa Verde National Park

In all, Mesa Verde has received funding for eight Vanishing Treasures positions. First, in 1998, two term masonry worker positions were converted to Subject-to-Furlough and filled by Kee Charley John and Willie Begay. Three years later, Willie retired and his position was filled by Neill Smith and three years after that, Kee retired and Exhibit Specialist Tim Hovezak was hired to fill the position.

In 2000, the park received additional base funding to create four new positions, a Historical Architect, a Database Archeologist, a Conservator, and a Structural Engineer.

The Historical Architect position was filled by Don Corbeil who left the position in March 2005. The funding for the historical architect was diverted to an Exhibit Specialist position held by Joel Brisbin.

The Database Archeologist position was originally held by Cynthia Williams Loebig who resigned in August of 2004. In 2005 the park filled this position with a GS-7 SCEP employee, Laura Ninnemann who was converted to a Subject-to-Furlough GS-7/9/11 Database Archeologist after her graduation in December 2005.

Unable to fill the Conservator position at the GS-11 level, the park hired Rebecca Carr as a Term GS-7 Conservator in 2001. The position was subsequently upgraded to a GS-9 and in April 2005, Rebecca accepted a permanent full-time position at Casa Grande National Monument. The park has recruited to hire a GS-11 Subject-to-Furlough Conservator but did not get any well-qualified applicants and the position remains vacant.

Preston Fisher was hired for the structural engineer position and continues to serve in an at-large capacity providing engineering consultation services to all VT parks.

In 2004, the park received funding for two additional Exhibit Specialists positions for the Stabilization Crew, which would have brought the crew total to five. We filled these positions with temporary personnel during 2004, and were able to fill one Subject-to-Furlough Exhibit Specialist position during 2005. Kay Barnett currently fills this position. The other position has not been filled.

Here are the accomplishments of Mesa Verde's VT staff during FY2005:

Joel Brisbin, Exhibit Specialist FY2000 Position
(converted in 2005)
Joel spends 100% of his time supervising the stabilization crew and the architectural documentation crew working on VT sites. In addition to his work at Mesa Verde, Joel and other park staff spent two weeks at Arch Canyon Ruin located in San Juan County, Utah. Under a multi-phase contract with the Bureau of Land Management, he assisted with the completion of level one architectural documentation of the site.

Tim Hovezak, Exhibit Specialist FY1998 Position
(converted in 2005)
Tim is not only a seasoned Southwestern archeologist, he also has years of experience working in the building trades and with structural stabilization. Tim is proving to be a valuable member of the Mesa Verde's stabilization crew.

Kay Barnett, Exhibit Specialist FY2004 Position Barnett is an experienced field Archeologist with over ten years of field and laboratory experience and three years of site stabilization work. Along with Joel, Kay spent two weeks at Arch Canyon Ruin in San Juan County, Utah assisting with the completion of level one architectural documentation of the site.

Kay supervised a crew of seasonals for the on-going, level one architectural documentation project at Spruce Tree House, which resumed after a year lay-off. This season's work began on the southern end of the site where our final 53 architectural units are to be found. Kay and the crew documented 29 of these architectural units including 17 rooms, one kiva, nine open areas, and two miscellaneous structures. This project was funded by a grant from the Colorado Historical Fund.

Neill Smith, Masonry Worker FY1998 Position
Beginning October 18, Neill Smith and Gary Ethridge
left for Lee's Ferry in the Glen Canyon National Recreation Area. This was a follow up visit for last year's work when numerous historical buildings were repaired. This two week stint was at the Lonely Dale Ranch historic site where they repaired portions of a slab and cement irrigation ditch.

Mesa Verde Stabilization Crew
For much of the field season, Joel, Tim, Kay and Neill work together as members of the Mesa Verde Stabilization Crew. While much of that crew is furloughed from Thanksgiving to the beginning of April, their first task last spring was to open the Chapin Mesa site shelters to ready them for summer visitation. This included raising the curtains around the mesa top road shelters, cleaning the associated drainage ditches and making small repairs to areas damaged over the winter months.

While these activities were somewhat routine, the next two projects were not. Inspections revealed that the two front country cliff dwellings on Wetherill Mesa, Step House, and Long House, had major problems that had to be addressed before the sites could be opened to the public.

At Step House, a 34 foot long section of the paved pathway inside the alcove had been undermined by running water and was beginning to slide downslope. After removing the damaged section, the old surface was replaced with tinted concrete, reinforced with wire, and placed on compacted soil. Repair work also included the replacement of deteriorated sections of the masonry retaining wall that holds the trail in place.

After completing the repairs at Step House, the crew moved across the mesa to Long House where a rock fall had been reported. Unfortunately, over the winter approximately seven tons of the alcove ceiling had fallen and crushed about half of the architecture of Kiva N. Eighteen days were required to

complete the repair work on Kiva N after which it was necessary to do some additional scaling in the area adjacent to the initial fall to secure the area near Kiva Q, where visitors congregate during tours

Once these major repairs were completed, the crew had just enough time to open the mesa top sites before Wetherill Mesa was opened to visitation.

With Wetherill Mesa open for the season, the focus of the team's efforts returned to Chapin Mesa where the winter snow had brought down two large walls at Far View House. Both walls had been scheduled for repair in 2005 but Mother Nature was in a hurry and the repairs had to be made sooner, rather than later.

Also on Chapin Mesa is the four story tower at Square Tower House. This tower was built in-part on loose fill, and rodent activity behind and under the southeast corner had caused a section of the masonry to subside and lean inward. After documenting the room, the technical problem of removing this wall without bringing the rest of the tower down had to be addressed. Working through the engineering, the bad section of wall was removed and large stones were used to create a solid footing. The original stones were then restacked in their original configuration atop the new footer. The original mortar was reconstituted and no foreign materials were introduced into the fabric of this structure.

In August, before closing down the Mesa Verde sites for the winter, the crew assisted with a 30 day project in Southeast Utah funded by Glen Canyon National Recreation Area. This work included the repair of three historic cabins in a remote area 50 miles northeast of Hanksville Utah.

Laura Ninnemann, Database Archeologist FY2000 Position
Laura continued work on the stabilization component of the Level 1/Level 2 database called ArcDocData. Revisions had been made to the prototype and its instructions following the 2004 field season and the revised field forms were tested during

the 2005 field season. Recommendations from the stabilization crew have been incorporated and final revisions to the database are to be completed during the 2006 field season.

Numerous revisions have been incorporated into both Level 1 and Level 2 field forms and their associated database objects in response to requests from the field crew. Revisions of this kind are time-consuming, albeit an important function of this position that is essential to maintaining a dynamic and responsive database.

In addition, forms and instructions for a new Structural Engineering component of ArcDocData have been designed in cooperation with Preston Fisher. Several revisions were made during the 2005 field season based on field testing by the new site survey and condition assessment field crews. As a result, the initial database design structure has been developed and it will be finalized during the 2006 field season.

Laura supervised a data entry crew of four individuals during the 2005 field season. Under her direction, the crew completed data entry for the new site survey and condition assessment crews, as well as the architectural documentation crew working at Spruce Tree House. Other supervisory duties included the review of site files for completeness prior to assignment, monitoring of work flow, post data-entry review, and integrity checks.

Laura is also working on an interface between the Level 1/Level 2 database and electronic data captured using Palm Pilots. The use of this technology will require an intensive inspection of existing database objects and field forms to assure that the data that is captured has a corresponding location within the database. In addition, pick lists must agree with the choices included on field forms, and data definitions must be properly structured. This work will continue through the 2006 field season.

Project Completion Reports
Continue Backcountry Condition Assessment Project – $130,500
In FY 2005, Mesa Verde received Vanishing Treasures funds to continue the Condition Assessment Project that was originated by the Vanishing Treasures Initiative in 1996. This project focuses on backcountry alcove sites, many of which have not been visited by archeologists since they were first recorded over 40 years ago. Two crews, of three archeologists each, evaluated the condition of alcove sites located within the backcountry of Mesa Verde National Park. Other positions that were funded by this project include a photographer and a data entry clerk.

This season, the project study area focused on continuing condition assessments at alcove sites that were affected by the 2002 Long Mesa Fire, and the 2003 Balcony House Complex fires. A total of 111 alcove sites were located within the combined fire perimeters. From our experience after other recent wildfires, alcoves within fire boundaries typically suffer accelerated condition problems due to increased overland runoff, ash and mud depositing on standing walls and features, accelerated mortar erosion, and increased instability due to spalling of building stones.

As a part of this project, each segment of standing architecture was assessed for damage from erosion, fire effects, and construction failure. Site documentation included mapping, photographing, condition assessment, collecting mortar samples, and completing a fire affects form packet.

A total of 24 alcove sites were documented using VT funds. The majority of the sites assessed were relatively small (1-10 units), while three large sites were documented: Hemenway House, Little Hemenway House, and Sunset House which contain 45, 18, and 24 rooms respectively, with multiple kivas. A total of 142 architectural units, including rooms, open areas, kivas, and a tower were assessed along with numerous rock modification panels. Of the 24 total sites that received condition assessment documentation, eight were recommended to receive more detailed architectural documentation, four for architectural fabric stabilization, two for water diversion tactics, and nine for further monitoring of their conditions. Five sites received a silicone dripline to help divert water from falling onto standing architecture and features. In addition, two sites that were considered at high risk for severe erosional threats were treated with excelsior matting and log diverters to help minimize accelerated water runoff.

Although not all of the sites involved in the fires have been assessed, those that are considered at most risk for post-fire erosional effects were documented between the FY04 and FY05 field seasons. There are 57 sites remaining which require condition assessments.

Budget:
Personnel: $118,683.82
Vehicles: $5,860
Travel/Training: $0
Supplies & Materials: $4,996
Equipment: $0
Services: $590
Other: $0
Total: $130,129.82
Balance: $370.18

Please note that we do not have the final printouts for FY05 so we believe these numbers are correct.
Base Funding in FY 2005: Mesa Verde did not receive any base funding increase in FY2005 to hire staff.
Base Funding in Previous Years: Mesa Verde did receive base funding for positions in FY 1998, 2000 and 2004.

Stabilization at Wolverton Cabin, Glen Canyon National Recreation Area; work performed by Mesa Verde Restoration Crew

Vanishing Treasures Parks in

New Mexico

Table 3.5. New Mexico Personnel Funding (In Thousands of Dollars)

	Aztec Ruins	Bandelier	Chaco Canyon	El Malpais	El Morro	Fort Union	Gila Cliff Dwellings	Pecos	Salinas Pueblo Missions	FY Total
FY 1998	84	0	0	0	0	0	0	0	33	84
FY 1999	4	113	214	68	0	0	0	0	148	399
FY 2000	0	0	0	58	0	0	0	0	55	58
FY 2001	58	0	55	0	55	0	0	0	0	168
FY 2002	0	0	55	0	0	71	0	0	0	126
FY 2003	0	0	0	0	0	0	0	0	126	0
FY 2004	0	0	0	0	0	0	0	0	0	0
FY 2005	0	0	0	25	0	82	0	0	0	107
Park Tota	146	113	324	151	55	153	0	0	362	*942*

Table 3.6. New Mexico Project Funding (In Thousands of Dollars)

	Aztec Ruins	Bandelier	Chaco Canyon	El Malpais	El Morro	Fort Union	Gila Cliff Dwellings	Pecos	Salinas Pueblo Missions	FY Total
FY 1998	75	0	113.3	0	0	0	0	0	25	213 3
FY 1999	63	0	125.5	0	0	0	0	0	10	198 5
FY 2000	0	0	110	0	0	30	0	0	95	235
FY 2001	0	0	125	0	0	40	0	69	417	275 7
FY 2002	0	50	125	7	8.9	0	0	40	116.4	347 3
FY 2003	0	76	125	0	0	0	109	0	118	428
FY 2004	0	120.5	109	0	0	0	8	0	119.3	356 8
FY 2005	19.5	0	110	74.2	0	0	45	0	123	3717
Park Tota	157 5	246 5	942 8	812	89	70	162	109	648 4	*2,426.3*

New Mexico Funding FY2005 (In Thousands of Dollars)

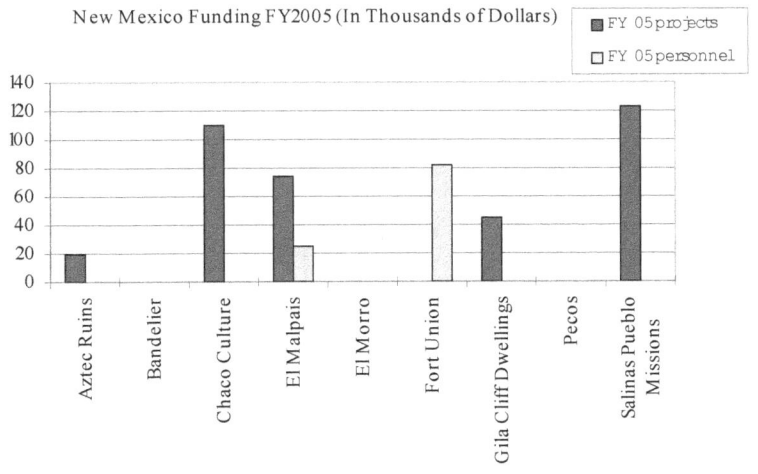

◆ Aztec Ruins National Monument

Raymond Torrivio and Carl Jim, Masonry Workers, FY 1998 Positions
These two stabilization experts continued work on several important preservation projects during FY 2004. Raymond is a permanent VT masonry worker, while Carl is a term employee who is funded both by VT and project funds. They provided essential direction for other project-funded preservation staff—Ernest Harrison and Mike Padilla. The crew accomplished considerable backfilling and minor ruins stabilization during field sessions in the fall of 2004 and spring/summer of 2005, along with routine preservation maintenance.

Backfilling was conducted around the eastern and northern exterior walls and in seven multi-story rooms at Aztec West Ruin. Five of these rooms required reversal of a 1982 backfill project so that drainage systems, soil retention structures, and other improvements could be installed. Re-excavation of these rooms also made it possible to conduct architectural and photographic documentation, and to collect wood samples for tree-ring and microbial analysis. The re-excavated rooms were then backfilled in accordance with the West Ruin Backfill project which has been ongoing since 1998. PVC drainages were installed in all of the backfilled rooms and connected with the existing exterior drainage systems.

Masonry repairs ranging from minor capping and repointing to stabilization were conducted in 22 rooms and one kiva at West Ruin. Carl served as masonry work leader. Work ranged from minor capping to extensive replacement of deteriorated sandstone and mortar. Digital photo-documentation and pre- and post-stabilization records were kept. The preservation crew also performed protective roof repairs in two rooms at West Ruin and two rooms at East Ruin; one major protective roof replacement project was initiated at West Ruin with VT project funds. In addition, routine ruins' maintenance tasks were performed throughout the year.

Training/ Technical Assistance provided:

Carl attended a VT stabilization forum held at SAPU in November 2004 which included discussions of issues and results of current preservation programs in northern New Mexico. Carl received Red Cross training in first aid and CPR. He and Raymond also participated in various on-line training programs during FY05.

Gary M. Brown, Archeologist, FY 2001 Position
Gary supervised both the preservation crew, funded mainly through VT, and an archeological crew that was hired with project funding. The survey crew conducted a comprehensive cultural resources inventory of AZRU and site condition assessments to address the servicewide corrective action plan. The preservation crew conducted work on backfilling, stabilization, protective roof repairs, and one VT project which addressed one major protective roof replacement. Five rooms that had been backfilled in 1982 were re-excavated and brought in line with the current backfill configuration. As suspected, the uncompacted alluvial sand that had been used for previous backfilling resulted in serious deterioration of masonry and wood features. In addition to these five rooms, two other multi-story rooms were backfilled during FY05. Gary continued to oversee pre-backfilling architectural and photographic documentation with the aid of three project-funded archeology technicians.

Preservation crew re-excavates 1982 backfill for drainage.

In addition to project work, Gary participated in the ongoing development of the park's General Management Plan and writing and review of PMIS proposals. He worked on a PMIS rating panel in Denver during February 2005, as well as various preservation activities at the park. He also participated in the successful submittal of research proposals to the National Science Foundation, the Western National Parks Association, and the Cooperative Ecosystem Study Unit. The NSF grant will fund architectural documentation at East Ruin in FY06 and FY07; the WNPA grant funded an outside researcher, during FY05, who completed backlogged analysis of perishable artifacts from a 1984 excavation at West Ruin; and the CESU cooperative agreement made it possible to launch a two-year hydrologic study at AZRU that began to address groundwater monitoring and mitigation of destructive effects on VT resources. Gary assisted the VT Program by participating in the VT Charter committee which reviewed and revised the 1998 draft charter. He also attended both the annual Pecos Conference and Society for American Archeology meetings, presenting a paper at the SAA based on architectural studies at West Ruin. He also gave several presentations on AZRU research to the general public.

Training/ Technical Assistance provided:

Gary attended several NPS training sessions during FY05: a VT preservation forum held at SAPU; an ASMIS and related NPS archeology workshop in Salt Lake City; New Mexico SHPO/NPS workshop in Aztec; and Fundamentals V in Harpers Ferry. He also conducted on-line training for PMDS, PEPC, PMIS, Fundamentals III and IV, Ethics, Safety, Supervision, Hazard Analysis, and numerous additional topics. Also during FY05, Gary updated his Red Cross training for certification in first aid and CPR.

Project Completion Reports

Replace Protective Roof and Bracing in Room 132 at Aztec's West Ruin - $22,955

Vanishing Treasures project and VT base funding made it possible to address a long-standing preservation problem in a two-story portion of the ancient West Ruin great house at Aztec Ruins. Room 132 is a first-story room with a completely intact original roof separating it from the second-story structure above, Room 133. For more than a century, the ground-floor room

has been plagued by excessive moisture due to leakage from above, capillarity from the surrounding masonry walls and adjacent fill, and inadequate ventilation to dehumidify the room. Some time in the 1940s, the National Park Service constructed a wooden protective roof above the ancient wood-and-earth roof, and poured a six inch thick concrete slab over the wooden protective roof. The weight of the concrete cracked several original vigas, requiring extensive bracing to support the roof system, and actually trapped moisture within the room underneath while sheltering the original roof from direct precipitation. Various roofing materials have been laid on the concrete roof over the years, but both leakage and capillary moisture have persisted.

The FY05 VT project included removal of the antiquated concrete roof and replacement with a more effective and lightweight protective roof system. Design of the new roof was assisted by Sayre Hutchison, VT Architect, and additional architectural experts in the Intermountain Support Office. Preston Fisher, VT Structural Engineer, served as Contracting Officer's Technical Representative and provided invaluable help with project implementation. The project was an outstanding collaboration of park, VT, and regional expertise, along with additional assistance from individuals at MEVE and Santa Fe. AZRU preservation personnel performed demolition of the existing roof, construction of a new wooden roof structure, and associated stabilization, while roof installation and details were outsourced to a local roofing contractor. Demolition and construction have been completed, and funding for the contract work has been obligated, but the actual work on roof installation will take place during early FY06. The project should be completed by the onset of winter weather.

Budget:
Personnel: $12,433.02
Vehicles: N/A
Travel/Training: N/A
Supplies and Materials: $5,422.07
Equipment: N/A
Services/Contracts: $9,058.29
Other: $426.59

♦ Bandelier National Monument

Angelyn Bass Rivera, FY 1999 Position

In FY05, Angelyn continued to co-direct the Vanishing Treasures (VT) Program with Architectural Conservator Mary Slater. FY05 field projects included the Frijoles Canyon Cavate Pueblo Conservation, Long House Pueblo Masonry Stabilization, and Documentation/Condition Assessment of the Backcountry Sites of Yapashi and San Miguel. This year the cavate conservation project included graffiti mitigation, medium-format and digital photography, laser scanning (Western Mapping, Inc.), monitoring of pilot conservation treatments, environmental monitoring, and scanning electron microscopy of plaster and paint samples. A detailed report on the project's accomplishments was written and sent to the Getty Foundation in completion of the Architectural Conservation Project Preparation Grant. Currently we are analyzing over five years of data on the Frijoles Canyon cavates and are preparing a formal conservation plan that defines significance and prioritizes cavate conservation treatments for the short- and long term.

In addition to field projects, Angelyn completed her responsibilities as COTR for the Tinware Project to conserve CCC-era decorative arts in the collection and in-use in the parks' historic district, and continues as COTR for the laser scanning project with Western Mapping. Angelyn submitted 9 SEPAS proposals for FY06-08 and participated in rating the VT projects. In the spring of 2005, The Peopling of Bandelier (SAR press) was released including a chapter written by Angelyn on the Frijoles Canyon cavate pueblos. Angelyn also co-edited and co-authored papers for the *The Conservation of Decorated Surfaces on Earthen Architecture: Proceedings from the International Colloquium organized by the Getty Conservation Institute and the National Park Service, 22-25 September 2004, Mesa Verde National Park, Colorado, USA* (published by the Getty Trust Publications; Spring 2006 release). In June, Angelyn gave a lecture to the Museum of New Mexico conservation staff on earthen plaster conservation.

Training/ Technical Assistance provided:
Fort Davis National Historic Site-Angelyn Bass Rivera and Lauren Meyer led a plaster stabilization and graffiti mitigation workshop for the University of Vermont Historic Preservation Field School, staff from other VT parks, and Ft. Davis personnel and volunteers

Angelyn worked 70% of full time in FY05 while pursuing an MBA at the University of New Mexico. Her remaining salary was used to support Lauren Meyer as the lead for the cavate project and other VT activities.

Mary E. Slater, Exhibit Specialist (Architectural Conservator), FY 1999 Position
Stabilization of masonry at Long House Pueblo, a 15th -16th century communal cavate pueblo in Frijoles Canyon. Long House was excavated by Edgar Lee Hewett in the first decade of the 20th century. The foundations of over 200 ground floor rooms have been maintained and stabilized by the NPS since 1932. Stabilization was carried out on 172 wall faces representing over 150 square meters of stone walls. Mary supervised the stabilization crew, which consisted of a term Exhibits Specialist and three Masonry Workers.

Documentation of three backcountry masonry pueblos. Yapashi Pueblo is a 14th century communal pueblo located on a mesa top near the center of the park. Containing approximately 170 exposed rooms, 19 rooms excavated by Hewett have been open since 1908. Frijolito Pueblo, a 15th century pueblo on the south rim of Frijoles Canyon, was also excavated and left open by Hewett in 1908. Frijolito has deteriorated to the point where there are no architectural remains visible. 93 masonry walls in the exposed rooms at Yapashi and San Miguel were photographed using a 35mm camera with black and white film. Detailed mapping at Frijolito will take place in early 2006. Because these sites are in backcountry areas and have not been stabilized, the recommended treatment is documentation and backfilling, though there are no funds to support backfilling at this time.

In addition to project work, Mary assisted the Pueblo of Santa Clara in preparing a successful grant application for preservation planning at Puye Village. Mary completed her responsibilities as COTR for a Save America's Treasures Project to conserve CCC objects and submitted the final report to SAT. She presented VT Program work to professional colleagues and the public in a paper at the 2005 US/ICOMOS Symposium. Mary wrote a book review for the Winter 2006 issue of *CRM: The Journal of Heritage Stewardship*. She also wrote eight SEPAS proposals and assisted in park planning for the rehabilitation of the historic Visitor Center, for which she conducted a paint analysis. Mary supported Park and program safety goals by writing four job hazard analyses pertaining to VT Program field work and by serving on a Safety Review Team involving a lost-time accident.

Training/ Technical Assistance provided:

Mary received training in the Facility Management Software System (FMSS) conducted July 11-15 at Bryce Canyon National Park.

Archeologist Rae Miller stabilizes the masonry walls in Long House, which were once multi-story rooms that fronted the cavates seen along the cliff face.

◆ Chaco Culture National Historic Park

Jack Trujillo, Leo Chiquito, Paul Tso, James Yazzie, and Lewis Murphy
Masonry Workers, FY 1999 and 2001
Positions

The Vanishing Treasures preservation staff worked on a variety of treatment projects ranging from condition assessments, architecture and treatment documentation, to significant preservation treatment at six of the front country structures in the park. The majority of work undertaken by the preservation staff this year was completing the Vanishing Treasures funded project to improve drainage and complete backfilling in Pueblo del Arroyo. This work is discussed at greater length in the park's Project Completion Report.

Over the winter, the staff worked in the darkroom to develop preservation photographs taken previously, labeling the photographs with the assistance of a museum technician, and completed written architectural and preservation treatment forms. Work schedules and scopes of work for field operations for the remainder of the fiscal year were established, and this information was incorporated into the compliance documents. Pre-treatment condition assessments were conducted to pinpoint the areas to be treated and to provide information on the quantity of materials that would be needed.

At Una Vida, a backfilled greathouse near the visitor center, wall capping and basal wall sections were found to be severely eroded by drainage from the talus slope above, which had been captured by the trail and subsequently funneled along the exterior wall. In addition, deteriorated interpretive stops were enabling visitors to trample wall tops. Similar problems were found at the unexcavated greathouse Hungo Pavi.

To address these problems, the trails at both of these structures were repaired early in the season. The capping was reset or replaced, drainage directed away from the structures, and areas of basal erosion repointed with soil mortars. Later in the season, the staff treated all of the vertical wall faces and wall capping that were found to be in poor condition at Talus Unit, a relatively small building that is adjacent to Chetro Ketl. Similar work was also necessary at Chetro Ketl, particularly on the central section of the building which has not been backfilled.

Other work performed by the Vanishing Treasures staff included the inspection and maintenance of all drainage features installed as part of the backfilling program; emergency repairs to the boundary fence wash crossings to prevent livestock from entering the park; emergency trail repairs after heavy rains; and monitoring conditions at the outlying units of Kin Bineola, Kin Klizhin, Kin Ya'a, and Pueblo Pintado.

James Yazzie, who serves as the lead photographer for the preservation crew, is responsible for the photo documentation of the treatment work. James has instructed several of the other crew members in the use of the shift lens and set-up requirements for this type of perspective-corrective architectural photography. All documentary photographs are taken in black & white, and several of the staff are now skilled in darkroom developing and printing. This allows film to be processed on-site to assure that the photographs are clear and that they accurately capture the work.

Training/   Technical   Assistance provided:
In November of 2004 the entire VT preservation crew participated in a seminar/workshop at Salinas Pueblo Missions to discuss preservation problems and solutions with other VT specialists in the region. During the course of the year, the preservation crew also took part in several types of safety training including Hazardous Materials Communication training and continued rock climbing training for preservation work on Fajada Butte and other cliff sites. The entire crew also attended, and was certified through the Scaffold Industry Association Training Program, in the use of tube and clamp scaffolding. This training was extremely valuable because of the complex scaffolding erections required for many of the backfilling, capping, and vertical wall treatments jobs, particularly at the large multi-storied structures and those in the cliff talus. Job Safety Analyses were completed for many of the routine activities associated with preservation treatment work. As a result of consultation with IMR Industrial Hygienist Jennifer Sahmel, the park maintains and monitors baseline and yearly hearing and respiratory fitness testing data.

Roger A. Moore, Archeologist, FY 1999 Position
Roger completed his second full year in the VT archeologist position, and has taken over supervision of the two staff members dedicated to the preservation documentation and archives programs. In FY 2005 Roger formalized the standards for architectural and treatment documentation for VT resources, and continuing development of electronic methods to store and

track compiled documentation. He worked closely with the park curator to structure the database so backlogged data from the past 30 years and current information can be entered into the system. Under Roger's supervision, a student working in the Albuquerque office of the Collections focused on the oldest of the preservation records, while an employee at the park worked in the more current backlog. Roger continued his experiments with mortar colors using cement based and soil based mortars, and conducted a number of tours and presentations that highlighted VT preservation activities for professional and avocational archeological organizations in the area.

Roger assisted with the daily operations of the preservation staff in both the backfilling and the wall treatment projects, and he maintains the ongoing structural and backfill monitoring program. Through this program, moisture levels are recorded at the monitoring ports in the Chetro Ketl backfill test area each month, and readings from the dial gage that monitors movement on the back wall of Pueblo Bonito are collect weekly. These and other monitoring data are maintained for long-term evaluations of preservation treatment and needs.

Roger worked closely with the University of New Mexico (UNM) researchers conducting a National Geographic Society funded excavation and field school at Pueblo Bonito. He assisted by coordinating and inspecting the excavations and the data collected, and he worked with the interpretive program to schedule volunteer work and visitor tours to the excavation site. In June, the park hosted a 2-day retreat for the New Mexico State Historic Preservation Office staff, discussing with them upcoming issues that will require close consultation, including the proposal by San Juan County to pave the access road into Chaco, the UNM excavations, backfilling and other preservation programs, and Native American consultation.

Training/ Technical Assistance provided:

In October and again in January, Roger attended the ARPA Condition Assessment and Archeological Law Enforcement training sessions, and is fully qualified to conduct and assess violations, which remain a persistent problem in the park. He attended the Society of American Archeology meetings in Salt Lake City, going early to participate in the NPS meeting and ASMIS/LCS training conducted prior to the regular sessions. Roger also represents the NPS on the Certification Council of the Archeological Society of New Mexico and is currently serving as chairman of that committee. As a representative of Chaco Culture NHP, Roger attended meetings of the Chaco Interagency Management Program.

FY05 Base funding for Chaco VT Program

The budget breakdown for FY 05 VT Base-Funded Preservation Staff is shown below:

5 Masonry Worker Conversion Personal Services: $224,544
Travel/Training: $ 713
Supplies/Equipment: $0

1 Archeologist intake Personal Services: $ 73,329
Travel/Training: $ 1,395
Supplies/Equipment: $ 3,620

Total VT Base Funding expended in FY05: $303,601

Project Completion Reports

Pueblo del Arroyo - $109,840

The funded FY05 VT project involved completion of backfilling and drainage repair in Pueblo del Arroyo, a large multi-storied great house in the core architectural area of the park. The size, vertical mass, architectural complexity, and location of the structure on the actively eroding banks of Chaco Wash complicated this backfilling and drainage project. This project began two years ago, with thorough documentation of the architecture, a conventional vibration analysis and a refraction survey to evaluate the subsurface stability beneath the foundations of the structure. These studies were incorporated into the Historic Structures Report which structured the scope of work for the backfill and drainage plan. Last year, the south 1/3 of the structure was backfilled, and drainage installed in about 35 rooms. Due to a serious accident with the generator, we were not able to complete the final six rooms in that section of the building.

This year, we began the final phase of the backfilling by completing those last six rooms in the south 1/3, and working on 45 rooms in the central section of the building. This work involved relatively complicated scaffolding and conveyor setups that spanned multiple second story rooms, extended the full length of the 10 conveyor sections, and included several complex drainage systems. Ten evaporative basins were set into deep rooms which could not be drained with conventional piping. Those rooms that could be drained with pipe required long outlet lines, one of which extended about 180 feet through the east plaza and into a drop structure used for the road drainage. This drain and several other outlet pipes required shallow trenching, mostly in disturbed fill, although intact archeological remains were discovered in an area beneath the old parking lot. An old vandal's trench which had been filled with historic trash from the 1900s-1910s era was used for the drainage, and with assistance from the University of New Mexico archeological field school, the park was able to conduct thorough investigations of these deposits, and install the drain with a minimum of disturbance to the resource. With these final drainages completed, and all the equipment removed, the staff spent the remainder of the time rehabilitating the work areas, replacing trail surfaces, and repositioning directional and interpretive signs.

Budget:
Personal Services: $83,470
Travel/Training: $3,018
Supplies/Equipment: $23,374
Total: $109,840

Pueblo del Arroyo, Room 37 on the left side of the photo has piping in place, a geotextile barrier covering the original surface, and is prepared for fill soil to be placed in the room. Room 41 on the right has been filled and final surface contouring will complete the treatment in this room.

◆ El Malpais National Monument

Jim Kendrick, FY 1999 ELMA Position
During FY 2005, Jim directed preservation projects at the Alben Homestead in El Malpais National Monument (funded by VT), Atsinna Pueblo at El Morro National Monument, and Puerco Ruin at Petrified Forest National Park. In addition to these projects, Jim established a new cooperative agreement with the University of Arizona to conduct architectural documentation and preservation planning at El Malpais' Earl Head Homestead. The Head Homestead dates to the early 1930s and contains one of the only log structures at El Malpais. Jim also renewed a cooperative agreement with Northern Arizona University to document Atsinna Pueblo at El Morro National Monument.

Calvin Chimoni, FY 2000 ELMA Position
This past year, Calvin worked on the Atsinna Pueblo Preservation Project at El Morro and assisted preservation masons working on the Alben Homestead (El Malpais NM) and Puerco Ruin (Petrified Forest NP) preservation projects. Calvin also was integral in conducting preservation maintenance activities at El Morro's North Atsinna Pueblo. He continues to develop and use unamended mortars, and has created a test panel at El Morro for this particular purpose. Calvin has also been very involved with developing safety procedures for preservation work at El Morro, El Malpais, and Petrified

Forest. This has contributed to an excellent safety record for the VT Program at these parks. As part of the SEPAS process, he participated in prioritizing preservation projects throughout the Intermountain Region.

Project Completion Reports
Alben Homestead Preservation Project-$73,902 Using Vanishing Treasures (VT) funds during Fiscal Year 2005, El Malpais staff saved the Alben Homestead from collapse. To enable the intact portion of the ruin to remain standing, the rapidly deteriorating residence of the late nineteenth to early twentieth century homestead (the oldest known within El Malpais National Monument) required preservation treatments this year. Initial efforts focused on high-resolution digital mapping and photo-documentation prior to treatment. The next phase of work involved transporting safety and preservation materials 1.6 km (1.0 miles) into the backcountry across rugged terrain of the Sandstone Bluffs. Preservation treatments included filling voids within the walls with both unamended mortar and sandstone (sandstone from Zuni was used in order to distinguish these new materials from the original fabric of the structure). In one area, collapsed building stones were reset based upon the monument's photo archives. The ruin is now in good condition and annual routine maintenance will be scheduled to begin in 2006.

Budget:
Personnel: $33,219.78
Vehicles: $11.51
Travel*: $4,366.54
Supplies: $5,185.16
Equipment: $7,582.81
Services/Contracts: $23.363.40
Other: $172.78
Total: $73,901.98

*WACC assistance

◆ El Morro National Monument

Vacant, 2001 ELMO Position: Preparing to advertise.
As El Morro National Monument balances preservation and financial sustainability, this position was vacant during FY 2005. The salary lapse, however, was used towards the preservation of Vanishing Treasures

resources (see table below). A majority (over 93%) of the funds were used for seasonal employees or towards achieving preservation goals through cooperative agreements (as facilitated by the Colorado Plateau Cooperative Ecosystem Study Unit). As a direct result of such an agreement with Northern Arizona University, El Morro has, for the first time, detailed architectural sheets of wall elevations at Atsinna Pueblo (the largest VT resource within the monument). Quite literally, every single rock has been digitally mapped on a significant number of rooms at Atsinna. The agreement established in FY 2005 will document the great kiva at Atsinna, a primary interpretive feature of El Morro. This documentation effort will provide baseline information for the VT program at El Morro and El Malpais. The products will also provide great interpretive tools for research and public education. El Morro is now well-prepared to advertise a permanent position again and will do so early in FY 2006.

Use of Lapse Funds:
Personnel: $13,122.28, Seasonal Mason
Vehicles: $1,428.89,   Fuel   and
Maintenance
Travel: $648.73
Contracts/Services: $38,234.85,
Cooperative   Agreement   with   NAU   to
document   Atsinna   Pueblo   (95%);
illustrator   for   ELMO   archeological
report (5%)
Supplies: $1,237.37
Other: $100.32, GSA Motor Pool
Total: $54,772.44

◆ Pecos National Historical Park

Although Pecos National Historical Park has no Vanishing Treasures funded positions and did not receive VT project funding, the staff there identified 42 high priority treatments needed on Vanishing Treasure resources that, if not done within the year, would likely have resulted in the loss of a significant amount of original fabric or significant features of these structures. In addressing those issues, the staff completed several tasks that improved the condition of Vanishing Treasure resources within the park. All of this work was paid for through ONPS base funding.

Of the 42 high priority repairs identifed, thirteen were completed in the Spanish Mission Convento, four in the 18th Spanish Mission Church, eight collapsed segments of the Defensive Wall were repaired, a stone wall section was replaced after being knocked out by vandals, and the base of the southwest exterior wall corner at Pigeon's Ranch Main Building was replaced and the facade stuccoed.

The Pecos NHP preservation crew is comprised of three less-than-full-time masonry workers and one half-time archeologist supervised by the full-time Cultural Resources Manager. The park was unable to tackle the remaining 21 high priority projects because of two permanent staff vacancies and a lack of project funding.

During August of 2005, two of our masonry workers attended the Vanishing Treasures workshop on lime plaster preservation at Fort Davis and both found this workshop both enjoyable and informative.

In an example of cooperative assistance, the park was able to provide technical assistance to Jemez State Park in developing a plan to construct a roof on a kiva in the Mission of San Diego.

◆ Salinas Pueblo Missions National Monument

Thelma Griego, Maintenance Worker (Ruins Preservation), FY 2003 Position
Thelma continued in her role as a key stabilization professional at Salinas Pueblo Missions National Monument. In 2005, Thelma, working side by side with the student hires performing hands-on stabilization, Thelma directed and instructed new hires on the principles and practices of ruins stabilization, and ensured a safe work environment. The season began at the Quarai Unit stabilizing the mission church and convento of *la Nuestra Señora de Purísima Concepción de Cuarac* (Quarai).

Thelma maintained daily logs of all materials used and work completed and participated in the park's annual vegetation control program.

Marc A. LeFrancois, Exhibit Specialist, FY 2003 Position

Working closely with VT Archeologist Phil Wilson, Marc continued to supervise the ruins stabilization team in their work on the mission convento of *la Nuestra Señora de Purísima Concepción de Cuarac* (Quarai); cyclic re-plastering of the Abó 19th century Spanish re-Settlement Structures; emergency stabilization of the 19th c. *Casa de Vallejos* at Abó and the 19th century *Casa de Gonzales* structure at Quarai; and the vegetation control program throughout the park. At Quarai, the mission convento was nearly completed, leaving only a small area before cold weather ended the season. A 19th century *ranchero* structure at Quarai also underwent emergency stabilization, protecting the building against imminent collapse. At the Abó site unit, the only remaining 19th century structure requiring emergency stabilization was completed, returning all structures at Abó to a fully stabilized condition, and back to a purely cyclic approach. The remaining three 19th century structures at Abó underwent cyclic repair, re-covering these structures with a sacrificial coat of adobe plaster, which protects the underlying historic fabric. Cyclic vegetation and site management occurred at all three of the park's site units, controlling plants that can potentially damage archeological resources. In addition to stabilization and site management duties, Marc also supervised a seasonal research assistant, a seasonal data-entry clerk, and two research volunteers.

Marc continued research on the Mound 7 backfilling project, collaborating with Steven DeVore of the NPS Mid-West Regional Office, and a team from the United States Geologic Survey (USGS) in Lincoln led by Lyndsay Ball, to conduct a deep-resistivity survey of Gran Quivira. The project covered the ten acres encompassing the immediate exhibition area in order to evaluate geologic anomalies, which in turn will help the park develop the best possible backfilling plan for the preservation of Mound 7 pueblo, as well as the subterranean resources. The park is now awaiting the final report, scheduled for completion in January 2006.

Working with VT Archeologist Tobin Roop, Marc served as one of the park's compliance officers, jointly completing a total of twenty compliance documents relating to stabilization, vegetation management, and the USGS survey, among others.

Other activities include Marc's continuing work on a historic structures report for the 19th century *Ranchero* structures at Abó, a park-wide historic resources study, and assisting Phil Wilson with managing the park's facilities management activities. Joining Phil Wilson, and Murt Sullivan of the park's interpretive staff, Marc presented the park's on-going stabilization and research projects to the *Friends of Tijeras Pueblo* at the USFS Sandia Ranger Station in Tijeras, New Mexico. Marc and Phil also presented at the *New Mexico Heritage Preservation Alliance* annual conference in Taos, New Mexico, again focusing on park activities and specifically on how the *Vanishing Treasures Program* has benefited New Mexico parks statewide. Marc is also volunteering his professional services to Fort Stanton, Inc., a burgeoning local group in Lincoln County, New Mexico that has as its mandate the preservation and interpretation of state-owned historic Fort Stanton. Marc is currently assisting the group by evaluating Building 7 of the fort, which will soon be undergoing adaptive reuse as an administration building and museum. Building 7 and the parade grounds of Fort Stanton was most recently used as a set for Episode V of Steven Spielberg's recent production, *Into the West*, using the fort to interpret scenes depicting the *Carlisle Indian School*.

Ramona Lopez, Maintenance Worker (Ruins Preservation), FY 1998 Position

Ramona continued in her role as a key stabilization professional at Salinas Pueblo Missions National Monument. In 2005, Ramona again served as an Assistant and Acting crew leader, supervising and training seasonal staff. Working side by side with her team doing hands-on stabilization, Ramona directed and instructed new hires on the principles and practices of ruins stabilization, and ensured a safe work environment. The season began at the Quarai Unit stabilizing the mission church and convento of *la Nuestra Señora de Purísima Concepción de Cuarac* (Quarai) and the historic Gonzales House. Ramona then moved to

Abó to stabilize *the Vallejos House* and assisting with the plaster coating of three 19th Century Spanish Reoccupation structures.

Ramona maintained daily logs of all materials used and work completed. Ramona continued to maintain an inventory of all stabilization equipment and supplies, and participated in the park's annual vegetation control program.

Tobin W. Roop, Archeologist, FY 2000 Position

During FY 2005, Tobin continued to manage a variety of cultural resource projects at Salinas. Tobin completed the Quarai backcountry cultural resources survey which identified three previously unknown VT resources. Architectural documentation and condition assessments were completed on these structures. Working in concert with Marc LeFrancois (SAPU Exhibit Specialist) and the SAPU stabilization crew, Tobin assisted in the development of a mud plaster utilizing historically accurate materials. Tobin also assisted in the stabilization of the *Vallejos House* at the Abó unit and application of a plaster coating to three 19th century Spanish reoccupation structures at the Abó unit.

Working with Marc Lefrancois (SAPU Exhibit Specialist) Tobin assisted in the completion of 20 compliance documents for park projects. Tobin continued to manage the parks museum collection, assisted in NAGPRA/Section 106 consultation meetings, and managed a backlog cataloging project of SAPU materials at Arizona State University. Tobin also updated the park's ASMIS database, and assisted with the updating and development of the park's stabilization database. Tobin attended NEPA/NHPA compliance training in Denver held by Intermountain Region.

Philip W. Wilson, Archeologist, FY 1999 Position

Phil continues to oversee the preservation program at Salinas Pueblo Missions, directing and reviewing preservation projects as well as associated planning, compliance and documentation activities. Specific accomplishments this year include: participating in the Facility Maintenance Software System (FMSS) archeology work group, looking at ways to integrate Heritage Assets into FMSS; serving as an instructor at a training session in Amman, Jordan sponsored by the Getty Institute and World Monuments Fund, for the Iraq State Board of Antiquities and Heritage staff; completing the Emerging Leaders Consortium, a Service-wide leadership training; representing the Vanishing Treasures Initiative by providing an overview presentation of the VT Program at the annual preservation conference of the New Mexico Heritage Preservation Alliance, "Preservation Pilgrimage – 05".

Phil also received the Intermountain Region Franklin G. Smith Award for Work Force Development and spent time writing preservation funding proposals, developing short and long-range preservation plans, and coordinating training for the Preservation Crew.

Project Completion Reports
San Buenaventura Mission Complex Ruins Planning- $150,776
Vanishing Treasures project funds for Salinas Pueblo Missions National Monument supported research, documentation and condition assessments of San Buenaventura Mission Complex ruins at the Gran Quivira Unit, with the intent of developing appropriate preservation treatments and strategies. The complex is affected by numerous previous stabilization episodes using Portland cement in high concentrations, and a variety of other physical and geologic impacts that required a thorough understanding before developing a treatment plan.

Funding components consisted of $68,500 to fund an inter-agency project with USGS to investigate, record and evaluate subsurface anomalies through deep-surface remote sensing techniques; $50,000 for three dimensional documentation and near-surface ground-penetrating radar; and $32,275.62 to fund supplies and staff time to perform photographic documentation, condition assessments, and data collection of all mission structures, and also to provide staff support for the remote sensing projects. NPS personnel on the project included 1 permanent and four term/seasonal employees who collectively worked approximately 500 hours. The New Mexico Bureau of Geology

and Mineral Resources performed some of the remote sensing, and collaborated and contributed to the USGS study and report, at no cost to the project.

The purpose of this documentation project is to study both above-ground and subsurface anomalies in order to better understand the overall dynamics of the site. This information is providing the park with the management tool it needs to determine the best treatment strategies for long-term preservation of the cultural resources at Gran Quivira. While the project focused on the mission ruins, in fact all of the resources at Gran Quivira will benefit from this study, especially the Mound 7 Pueblo, of which the subsurface dynamics are clearly a major impact upon the pueblo's long-term preservation. The objectives identified for this fiscal year were accomplished in full.

Other 2005 projects supported through Vanishing Treasures staffing include the cyclic replastering of three 19th century Spanish settlement casas at the Abó site unit, the emergency stabilization of a fourth Abó casa, the emergency stabilization of a Spanish settlement casa at the Quarai site unit, and continued cyclic stabilization on the Quarai mission.

Basal erosion of the adobe shelter coat on the north wall and chimney of Gachado Line Camp located just north of the border with Mexico in Organ Pipe Cactus National Monument.

V a n i s h i n g   T r e a s u r e s   P a r k s   i n

T e x a s

Table 3.7. Texas Personnel Funding (In Thousands of Dollars)

	Big Bend	Fort Davis	San Antonio	FY Total
FY 1998	0	0	0	0
FY 1999	0	0	71	71
FY 2000	0	110	55	165
FY 2001	0	0	0	0
FY 2002	0	0	0	0
FY 2003	0	0	72	72
FY 2004	0	0	70	70
FY 2005	0	0	0	0
Park Tota	0	110	268	*378*

Table 3.8 Texas Project Funding (In Thousands of Dollars)

	Big Bend	Fort Davis	San Antonio	FY Total
FY 1998	0	0	0	0
FY 1999	10	0	0	10
FY 2000	0	0	0	0
FY 2001	0	39	64 5	103 5
FY 2002	49	39 1	0	87 9
FY 2003	0	0	0	0
FY 2004	0	0	0	0
FY 2005	0	44 1	0	44 1
Park Tota	58 8	122 2	64 5	*245.5*

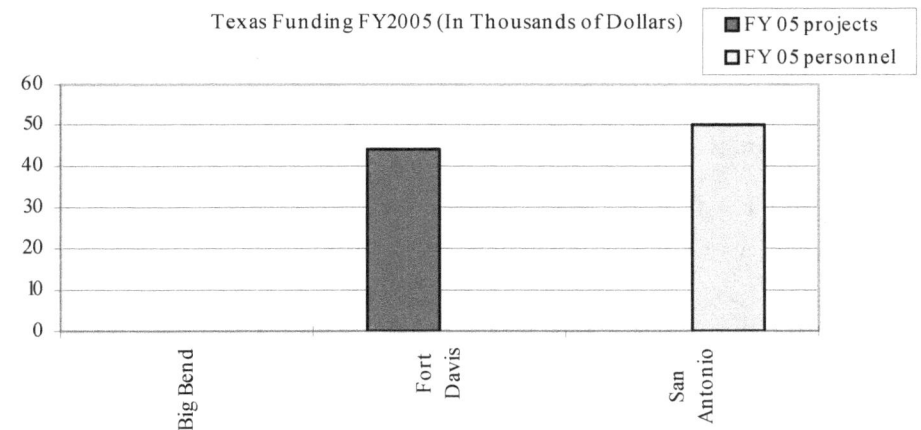

Texas Funding FY2005 (In Thousands of Dollars) — ■ FY 05 projects ☐ FY 05 personnel

Fort Davis National Historic Site

Jeffrey Rust, Cultural Resource Manager, FY 2000 Position
In FY 2005, Jeffrey Rust continued to manage the cultural resource activities and historic preservation projects at the park. In FY2005, the Cultural Resource and Facility Divisions of the park were combined into one division, with Jeffrey Rust as the Program Manager of the newly created division.

His accomplishments in FY2005 include preservation planning to evaluate and design treatments for future projects; supervising seven permanent employees and six seasonal employees; overseeing the Facility Management Program (FMP); overseeing the Facility Management Software System (FMSS) for the park; planning and supervising the park's YCC program; ensuring quality control of historic preservation projects; documenting historic preservation projects and treatments; evaluating and monitoring over 130 historic structures at the site; supervising and overseeing the museum curation program at the park; implementing the park's cultural landscape program; completing environmental and cultural compliance documentation; and ensuring that all park projects and treatments involving historic structures comply with the Secretary of the Interior's Standards for the Treatment of Historic Properties.

Roy Cataño, Masonry Worker, FY 2000 Position
In FY2004, Roy Cataño functioned as the work leader of five employees during preservation treatments on two historic adobe structures at Fort Davis. Both the post cavalry corrals (HB-41) and the two-story officers' quarters (HB-15) are contributing components of Fort Davis National Historic Landmark. The stabilization treatment on the cavalry corrals consisted of capping the exposed walls with adobe bricks amended with white Portland cement. The stabilization treatment on the two-story officers quarters consisted of repairing/rebuilding a collapsed lateral adobe wall with unamended adobe bricks and keying them in to the existing center wall to reduce differential swaying of the center wall. The tops of exposed adobe walls

on this ruin were also capped with adobe bricks amended with white Portland cement and pointed with a lime and sand mortar to match the original. All bricks used in these treatments (both amended and unamended) were made to match the original adobe bricks in size, texture, color, and shape.

Roy also assisted with plaster stabilization and repair of the Post Hospital (HB-46) during the three week Historic Preservation Field School with the University of Vermont Graduate Program in Historic Preservation.

Use of Lapse Funds:
Because Roy Cataño's position is subject to Furlough, he was financed for six months from Vanishing Treasures funds and for five months from project funds. The lapsed salary from his work schedule reduction was then used to partially fund an existing permanent WG-7 maintenance worker at the park (Ramon Sanchez) who assisted with historic preservation projects.

Plaster Stabilization in the Hospital Stewards Quarters at Fort Davis.

Project Completion Reports
Post Hospital Restoration Project - $44,100
In an excellent example of partnering and leveraging of VT dollars, Fort Davis NHS was able to work with the University of Vermont's Graduate Program in Historic Preservation to set up a three week historic preservation field school to work on the Post Hospital. With assistance from Jake Barrow, Exhibit Specialist from the Santa Fe Support Office, Vanishing Treasures funds were utilized in conjunction with an ongoing Save America's Treasures grant to fund the

Post Hospital Restoration Project. The preservation field school consisted of three parts: 1) stabilization and repair of the interior lime plasters, 2) in-kind reproduction and replacement of three historic windows, and 3) in-kind construction and replacement of interior flooring. The field school focused on historic preservation training and documentation of the resource before and after treatments. Training in plaster stabilization was provided by Vanishing Treasures Archeological Site Conservator Angelyn Rivera and Exhibit Specialist Lauren Meyer, and training in plaster replacement was provided by Pat Taylor of Cornerstones Community Partnerships. The project was an incredible success with over 20 staff, students, and volunteers participating during the week of plaster stabilization and repair. Over 1,000 hours of donated time were contributed to the project in conjunction with the field school.

Budget:
Personnel: $1,630
(Temp GS-5 Archeology aids – Mapping plaster)
Vehicles: $426
Travel: $1,200
Supplies and Materials: $12,688
Contracts: $25,028
(University of Vermont Field School)
Contracts: $3,128
(Cornerstones Community Partnerships)
Total: $44,100

Wall capping at Fort Davis

Vanishing Treasures Parks in

Utah

Table 3.9. Utah Personnel Funding (In Thousands of Dollars)

	Arches	Capital Reef	Canyonlands	Glen Canyon	Golden Spike	Hovenweep	Natural Bridges	Zion	FY Total
FY 1998	0	0	0	0	0	0	0	0	0
FY 1999	0	0	0	0	0	0	0	0	0
FY 2000	0	0	0	0	0	0	0	0	0
FY 2001	0	0	0	0	0	0	0	0	0
FY 2002	0	0	118	63	0	70	0	0	251
FY 2003	0	0	0	0	0	75	0	0	75
FY 2004	0	0	0	0	0	0	0	0	0
FY 2005	0	0	0	0	95	0	0	0	95
Park Total	0	0	118	63	95	145	0	0	*421*

Table 3.10. Utah Project Funding (In Thousands of Dollars)

	Arches	Capital Reef	Canyonlands	Glen Canyon	Golden Spike	Hovenweep	Natural Bridges	Zion	FY Total
FY 1998	0	0	0	0	0	0	0	0	0
FY 1999	0	0	0	55	0	10	0	0	65
FY 2000	0	0	100	20	0	0	0	5	125
FY 2001	0	0	0	115	0	30	0	0	145
FY 2002	0	0	56 4	0	0	24	0	0	80 4
FY 2003	0	0	0	0	0	0	0	0	0
FY 2004	0	0	0	0	50	0	0	45 3	95 3
FY 2005	0	0	0	0	0	0	90	39 4	129 4
Park Total	0	0	156 4	190	50	64	90	89 7	*640.1*

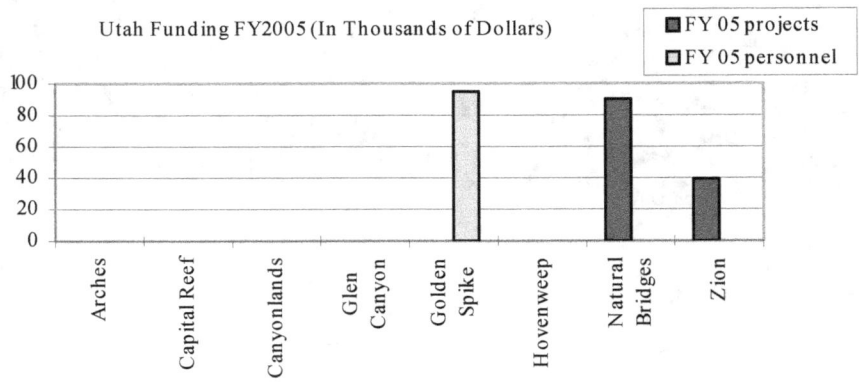

Utah Funding FY2005 (In Thousands of Dollars)

- FY 05 projects
- FY 05 personnel

♦ Canyonlands National Park

Melissa Memory, Archeologist, FY 2002 Position

In FY2005, Melissa Memory continued to oversee a multi-year project to document and perform condition assessments on Vanishing Treasures resources along the Colorado and Green River Corridors in Canyonlands National Park. This project is the first to be conducted by the Southeast Utah Group's Ruins Preservation Program. Field methodologies for documentation, condition assessments, and subsequent monitoring have been developed, and databases have been designed that will be used for cultural resource activities in all of the units of the Group. Melissa also participated in the Bare Ladder Ruin Documentation and Condition Assessment project at Natural Bridges National Monument.

Pat Flanigan, Exhibit Specialist, FY 2002 Position

In FY 2005, Pat Flanigan spent much of his time performing site documentation and updating condition assessments on Vanishing Treasures resources. He updated data and acquired determinations of eligibility for six sites listed on the Arches National Park LCS and entered associated information into ASMIS and the LCS database. In addition, he documented five new sites in the Horseshoe Canyon detached unit of Canyonlands National Park and entered associated information into the park and ASMIS databases. He also monitored nine Vanishing Treasures sites in Arches National Park and eight sites in the Island-in-the-Sky District of Canyonlands National Park, updating data, performing condition assessments, and entering the associated information into the park and ASMIS databases.

Pat participated in the River Corridor Architecture and Rock Art Survey in Canyonlands National Park, and the documentation and condition assessment at Bare Ladder Ruin in Natural Bridges National Monument. He also supervised a crew from the Canyon Country Conservation Corps on projects in the Needles District and Island-in-the-Sky Districts of Canyonlands National Park.

♦ Glen Canyon National Recreation Area

Lynn Wulf, Archeologist, FY 2002 Position

The permanent VT position was vacant during much of 2005; lapse funds were used to cover Lynn's salary during this time. This is the third fiscal year in which Lynn, while employed in a temporary position, continued to fulfill primary responsibilities for VT projects as well as developing and implementing new operating procedures to fulfill VT program management needs. February was the last month of her temporary appointment and in August she filled the permanent VT position.

In FY 2005 Lynn worked on two long-term preservation projects. The Lonely Dell Irrigation Ditch Restoration project was implemented from April through September FY04, and Lynn completed final documentation in FY05. This work included completing feature descriptions, photographic documentation, mapping, and preparing the final project report. She also coordinated with and assisted Tim Windle, Park Civil Engineer, to complete a detailed AutoCAD map of the southern half of the ditch. Lynn also assisted in coordinating contract completion requirements, logistics and staff support for the Mesa Verde Stabilization crew during the Wolverton Cabin Stabilization.

Additional on-going VT project responsibilities included coordinating with Northern Arizona University for structural sites in the Escalante River system, to complete Phase I of a condition assessment project. This first phase of the project included condition assessments (Level 2 documentation) for 39 features present at 21 sites, and documenting architectural remains (Level 1 documentation) for 32 of the features at 19 of those sites. She also continued working on the development of the monitoring and condition assessment program, database update and management, and fine-tuning the database management system.

Finally, Lynn continued working in the park and with IMR and WASO to identify management strategies for sites subjected to repeated and irregular inundation episodes. Field visits have confirmed that some sites containing drylaid structures and features, as well as lithics and sherds, can be in unexpectedly good condition and should not be designated as destroyed due to inundation alone. This poses a management identification problem in the ASMIS database and requires WASO concurrence, since it could affect multiple parks with sites recorded in and around lakes and reservoirs.

Training/ Technical Assistance provided:

In September, Lynn attended two intensive ESRI ArcGIS training sessions in Flagstaff, Arizona. This training will be used to design Geodatabases, joined and linked with primary archeological sites databases (ASMIS, IMACS, etc), photographs, site associated documents and maps.

Judy Huether, GIS Specialist

Vanishing Treasures funds were used for one pay period for Judy to evaluate and facilitate the reorganization of Park GIS VT databases and to complete metadata updates.

Equipment:

To address long-term goals of upgrading the VT documentation capability, VT money was used to purchase a variety of equipment related to mapping and recording efforts. New software was purchased enabling plan, elevation and isometric drawings to be produced from photographs. The drawings can be converted to AutoCAD drawings, which should prove to save office and field time. These products can in turn be brought into ArcGIS projects. Computer capability was also increased with the purchase of an oversize color printer and an expanded monitor.

Budget:
Personnel: $22,764
(Lynn Wulf $20,677)
(Judy Huether $2,087)
Vehicles: $0
Training: $2,250
Travel: $506
Supplies and Materials: $2,691
Equipment: $5,672
Services (Contracts, etc): $0
Other: $1,940
(Administrative Services)

Project Completion Reports
Condition Assessments in the Escalante River System, Progress Report- $27,468

In FY 2005 work continued on phase 1 of a two phase CPCESU contract with Northern Arizona University for the condition assessment of structural sites in the Escalante River canyon system. Objectives for this project included 1) to perform detailed documentation and condition assessment on selected structural sites; 2) to utilize site information to understand the nature and distribution of structural site types; and 3) to develop stabilization needs and priorities based on condition information and increased understanding of site variability and distribution within the canyons.

Project activities included completing detailed documentation (Level 1) for 32 structures at 19 sites, as well as condition assessments (Level 2) at 21 sites containing 39 structures. Nine of the 21 sites receiving Level 2 documentation had not previously received formal recordation. All site condition assessments included artifact inventories and detailed maps and photographs. In additional to the project, four sites were visited, photographed, and evaluated for eligibility inclusion under the criteria for this condition assessment project.

The majority of structures documented consisted of detached granaries, often occurring apart from other remains in isolated and hard to reach locations. These granaries exhibited a wide variety of materials, features, sizes and designs; the relationship between granary styles and the Basketmaker-to-Pueblo III occupation of the area was unknown. In order to guide management decisions, we attempted to develop information to test for patterns in the occurrence of various granary types through time.

Twenty-four organic specimens suitable for dating specific features were collected; analysis focused on seven samples which represented the range of observed architectural types. Results suggested a regular stylistic progression from Basketmaker II through Pueblo I time periods, beginning with circular alluvial cists, progressing to upright slab-lined cists with a variety of features, to increasingly complex masonry construction. Later period occupations were not reflected within the sample.

A synthesis report was produced containing research results, condition data, site forms, profile and plan view maps, photographs, carbon dating analysis, and treatment and management recommendations with priorities. In addition, NAU staff developed structure and variables for a new VT Access database containing information on construction details, condition assessment results, and recommended actions.

Wolverton Cabin Stabilization Project- $45,000

In FY 2005 the Wolverton Cabin Stabilization Project was completed. The structures at this site were built around 1919 by Edwin T. Wolverton, a prominent local engineer, prospector and entrepreneur who also constructed the elaborate Wolverton Mill now located in Hanksville; and Lou Chaffin, a stone mason who constructed several buildings in the region, including the Torrey schoolhouse which is currently on the National Register of Historic Places. This site consists of two cabins- a single room stone structure and a log and stone structure with an attached stone root cellar. It is the largest structural site in the northern portion of the park, is on the List of Classified Structures, and is part of a planned National Historic Register District.

Although remote, this site is frequently visited by backpackers and backcountry enthusiasts, and represents a substantial interpretive resource. Until recently, these uniquely constructed cabins remained in unusually good condition, and had never been stabilized prior to this project. The larger room of the 2-room structure is constructed of an interior and exterior log veneer, with a dirt and rubble core; this construction style is highly unusual although perhaps not surprising given the skill exhibited by Wolverton and Chaffin on other construction projects. The peaked roof, which extended over the adjoining masonry root cellar, was constructed of massive juniper and pinyon beams supported on the uphill by a masonry stem wall built into a bedrock outcrop. Unfortunately, during the winter of

2002 the failure of the supporting masonry stem wall, together with deterioration of some of the primary beams, led to the collapse of the roof. Left untreated, loss of both structures would have been inevitable.

Stabilization work was completed by the stabilization crew from Mesa Verde National Park. In the process, the entire roof was disassembled, the masonry stem wall was rebuilt, and the roof beams were replaced using new, stronger beams where necessary. Following the original roof construction exactly, secondary juniper poles were added and intervening spaces filled with large quantities of juniper bark. Finally, several inches of dirt were added over the entire roof surface. Minor repairs were also completed on the log and rubble wall components of the main structure, masonry components of the root cellar, and window and door frames of both structures. A small amount of work was also completed on the single stone cabin, which is in an advanced state of deterioration due to an intense fire that destroyed its wood components.

Detailed documentation was completed during all stages of the project, including plan maps and photographs. In addition, GLCA has contracted for AutoCAD plan and elevation maps to be completed for all three structures, along with an electronic interactive report. These will provide a basis for recording work completed during the course of the stabilization project, as well as future monitoring and stabilization efforts.

♦ Golden Spike National Historic Site

Bret Guisto, Archeologist, FY 2005 Position

Bret was hired as the park's Vanishing Treasures archeologist during the summer of 2005. Bret has a broad background in archeology and for the past 14 years, he has worked on numerous projects in academic, private and federal sectors. He received a BA degree in archeology from Simon Fraser University in 1995 and an MA in anthropology from the University of Victoria in 2003. Prior to his position at Golden Spike National Historic Site, Bret was an archeologist for the Salmon-Challis and Sawtooth

National Forests and Lake Mead National Recreation Area. While his academic studies and field work have taken him around the globe, the Great Basin and its cultural transition zones has become the core of his professional focus.

Bret quickly became familiar with the park's cultural resources and began identifying future needs, as well as needs related to ongoing projects. He completed the biannual grade survey this fall and plans to spend the winter preparing for field projects this spring, including evaluation of several archeological sites and continuing stabilization and preservation efforts on several historic structures.

Use of Lapse Funds:
Because Golden Spike has never had an archeologist and was adding an additional staff member, the park did not have any infrastructure or equipment (not even an office space or phone line) to support the position. Thus, a substantial amount of start up cost was incurred. Lapsed funds were used to create and furnish an office for the archeologist, as well as to purchase basic supplies and equipment needed to effectively accomplish VT program goals. Lapsed funds were also used to pay PCS costs. The park incurred an additional cost of almost $1,000 above VT funding to support this position. A breakdown of expended funds appears below.

Budget:
Personnel: $14,771.23   (permanent salary)
Vehicles: $358
Travel /Training: $0
Supplies: $17,675.82
Equipment: $25,369.05
Services: $4,189.82
Other: $33,564.58 (PCS)
Total: $95,928.50

♦ **Hovenweep National Monument**

Laura Martin, Exhibit Specialist FY2004 Position
Laura was selected at the end of FY 2004 to fill the VT Exhibit Specialist position previously vacated by Fred Gomez for the Southeast Utah Group. She is currently duty-stationed at Hovenweep National Monument, where she assists in preservation projects

occurring at Hovenweep National Monument, Natural Bridges National Monument, Arches and Canyonlands National Park. Laura has a B.A. in anthropology from the University of Cincinnati, and has worked professionally as an archeologist since 1993. Her employment with the National Park Service began in 1997 when she participated in the Dome Fire Archeological Project in Bandelier National Monument. In the fall of 1997 she was hired by Mesa Verde National Park to perform post-fire damage assessments and documentations, and to develop and implement treatments for sites that were threatened by post-fire accelerated erosion. In 2000, she continued at Mesa Verde as part of the Save America's Treasures Project / Archeological Site Conservation Program where she held a supervisory archeologist position responsible for leading crews in conducting condition assessments and treatments of architectural sites within the back-country. During 2001, at Mesa Verde, Laura took on the responsibility of developing new mapping protocols to improve the integration of architectural documentation products. She continued this effort at Canyonlands National Park, when in 2004 she accepted a term position responsible for the development and implementation of mapping protocols for the Southeast Utah Group's Baseline Architectural Documentation and Condition Assessment Program. These protocols were developed to streamline architectural documentation and pre-stabilization documentation at sites targeted for fabric interventions, as well as to contribute important control in baseline conditional data.

In FY 2005, Laura carried over her mapping responsibilities to her new position to assist in the documentation and condition assessment of VT resources within the high visitor-use area of the river corridors of Canyonlands National Park. She also conducted condition assessments of standing architecture, and made recommendations for treatment and stabilization to VT resources. She also assisted in conducting condition assessments at Bare Ladder in Natural Bridges National Monument, where she took part in a partnership program with the Hopi Foundation by instructing members in GPS and Total Station mapping methods. She continues to develop improvements to mapping methods used to document architectural sites and is currently developing mapping products to assist in architectural documentation and monitoring of VT resources within the SEUG parks.

Noreen Fritz, Archeologist, FY 2003 Position
During FY 05 Noreen conducted a variety of projects related to the Vanishing Treasures program. In an excellent example of inter-park resource sharing and collaborative partnership, Noreen acted as the Project Director for a VT-funded effort to update the documentation and condition assessments on multiple structures at Bare Ladder Ruin in Natural Bridges National Monument. This was a very successful collaborative effort between the National Park Service and the Hopi Foundation, a non-profit organization dedicated to self sufficiency, proactive community participation and self reliance for the Hopi people.

Noreen also took on the task of updating the documentation for 13 List of Classified Structure (LCS) records at Hovenweep National Monument and two LCS records at Natural Bridges National Monument. Most of the sites selected had not been updated since the early 1970s. Architectural documentation and updated condition assessments were performed at each of the sites, SHPO concurrence on eligibility was obtained, the data was entered into the LCS, ASMIS, and park-based databases, and all of these sites are now certified.

Noreen also participated in a number of additional projects including assisting a contractor in an effort to document and perform condition assessments at nine newly-discovered architectural sites in the Maze District of Canyonlands National Park. She was the co-lead on a Sierra Club work trip, assisting participants in the documentation and condition assessments of a number of sites in the Needles District of Canyonlands National Park. She also made frequent trips to the Goodman Point Unit of Hovenweep National Monument to monitor and participate in the on-going testing project that Crow Canyon Archeological

Center is undertaking in partnership with Hovenweep National Monument.

◆ Natural Bridges National Monument

Project Completion Reports
Perform Level I and II Documentation at Bare Ladder Ruin -$90,000
Documentation and condition assessment was performed at Bare Ladder Ruin in Natural Bridges National Monument. Bare Ladder contains a total of 60 structures and is the largest and most complex prehistoric site within the Monument. It was originally documented and stabilized in 1985 but no additional work had been done since that time and the site had been experiencing heavy visitation over the last few years. The project was designed to determine current architectural conditions at the site in anticipation of the need for preservation treatments in the very near future.

This Vanishing Treasures-funded project was accomplished in partnership with the Hopi Foundation, a non-profit organization that promotes self sufficiency, proactive community participation and self reliance for the Hopi people. The Foundation provides Hopi youth with training opportunities in the areas of cultural resource preservation and restoration. Eight Hopi tribal members representing several villages from all three mesas participated in the project.

Prior to the beginning of fieldwork, Project Director and Vanishing Treasures Archeologist Noreen Fritz spent a week at the Hopi mesas providing training to the participants. Once on site, the four weeks of project work consisted of structure-by-structure condition assessment, documentation, photography, and mapping. The numerous rock art panels at this site were also completely mapped and documented. The final week was again spent at Hopi debriefing the participants and discussing other collaborative opportunities.

Budget:
Personnel: $27,778
Vehicles: $3,174
Travel/Training: $1,192
Supplies and Materials: $2,237
Equipment: $2,469

Services: $51,658
Other: $1,493
Total: $90,000

◆ Zion National Park

Project Completion Reports
Document and Prepare Treatment Strategies for Sites in Parunuweap Canyon -$38,131
Funding
Requested: $39,400
Expended: $38,131
Balance: $1268.69
Note: The remaining balance occurred due to personnel changes that occurred within the last programmed pay period of FY05.

Budget: (as per AFS3
Personnel: $29,771.21
Vehicles: $3838.96
Travel $525.05
Supplies $3894.80
Equipment: $0
Services: $0
Other: $101.29
Total: $38,131.31

Note: This project has been partially funded in FY05 with the remainder of funding to be received in FY06. Accomplishments reported here are accordingly for only part of the project. The remainder and bulk of field work and the final report and treatment plan will be completed in FY06.

The abundance and exceptional condition of prehistoric sites in Parunuweap Canyon led to its inclusion in Zion when it became a National Park in 1918. In the 1930s, Civil Works Administration (CWA) crews excavated six sites within Parunuweap Canyon but neglected to backfill the structures leaving them vulnerable to accelerated deterioration. In addition, vandalism and such visitor use as guided horse tours have also heavily impacted many of the sites. Some of these pressures eased when the canyon was designated as an archeological district in the National Register of Historic Places in 1996, and then managed as a Research Natural Area (RNA) beginning in 2000.

Although some sites were recorded sporadically between 1933 and 1986, it was not until the early 1990s that all of the sites in Parunuweap Canyon were identified and recorded. The documentation conducted at this time was minimal, consisting only of the standard Intermountain Antiquities Computer System (IMACS) form. No condition assessments, preservation recommendations, or treatments were completed.

Minimal condition assessments and stabilization were conducted on six of the sites in 1994 and 1995. Since that time however, no further work has been conducted and monitoring crews (in the field very sporadically) have noted continuing deterioration of both stabilized and unstabilized features.

Documentation of alcove site in Zion

With Vanishing Treasures funding, archeologists returned to the canyon in FY 2005 to conduct systematic architectural documentation of extant masonry features at a number of the project sites and additional architectural documentation field work is planned for FY 2006.

As a result of this year's work, we have determined that documentation and preservation treatments at these sites are needed primarily because of natural processes exacerbated by human caused impacts. Because Parunuweap Canyon is narrow, steep sided, and highly geologically active, erosional processes work rapidly on the natural landscape to produce the usual and expected impacts on these sites. However, because the excavated sites were never backfilled but left exposed for over 60 years, these natural erosive effects have been amplified, resulting in many features reduced to a degraded state.

VT project funding was used to hire three seasonal archeologists who conducted extensive archival research to document and compile past activities and treatments at all of the project sites. As a result, the park now has a complete and easily accessible record of all documented activities for each site that is cross-referenced with pertinent documents and objects with Automated National Catalog System (ANCS) accession numbers and document locations. Information gaps were identified and rectified, and missing objects located.

New data collected this season have been entered into the Zion Architectural Documentation database, a specially designed MicroSoft Access based program. Newly recorded information includes a formatted, detailed feature description, current condition information, and treatment recommendations. In addition, architectural documentation was used both as a form of treatment for the project sites and to provide a comprehensive record of physical treatments. Inaccuracies and deficiencies in the original site recording were rectified with this architectural documentation data. Site locations are now accurately documented through systematic GPS position collection and existing cultural site coverages

have been updated. A new GIS coverage was created for each site with attribute data that will specifically track existing and future conditions and preservation treatment needs. Systematic photography of the sites will provide clear, concise imagery that establishes reference conditions for each feature. Legacy data, consisting of the original IMACS forms, have been updated.

The final product of this project will be preservation plans and treatment recommendations that will be developed as part of the final report to be completed in FY 2006. Along with specific treatment recommendations for site features, a key element of the long-term preservation plan will be regular and consistent monitoring. Zion's Archeological Site Monitoring program will facilitate this effort, assuring that appropriate documentation is maintained and that the sites are preserved.

Documentation was completed for 10 of the 15 project sites in FY 2005, the remainder (including the largest site) will be documented in FY 2006.

Team Documentation in alcove site in Zion

Vanishing Treasures Parks in

Wyoming

◆ Fort Laramie National Historic Site

Fort Laramie National Historic Site was established by Presidential Proclamation in 1938.   Fort Laramie was a key military fort on the western frontier and played a vital role in the westward overland migrations to Utah, Oregon, and California, with over 350,000 pioneer emigrants passing through on numerous trails using Fort Laramie as an essential point of supply, security and communication.

Many of the original 1800's buildings and structures exist today and still contain a high degree of original fabric. These buildings are surrounded by a remarkably unaltered historic landscape and view shed. Allowing visitors a nearly unprecedented opportunity to visit and experience not only an historic place, but also an historic environment. Fort Laramie NHS represents a priceless collection of early Western Military Architecture and little altered open space.

Although Fort Laramie National Historic Site does not have a funded position, Exhibit Specialist Donald

Icehouse foundations

LeDeaux is serving on the Vanishing Treasures Advisory Group and has been appointed Chairman of the Advisory Group's Training Committee.

Fort Laramie Hospital

Terminology

Definition of Vanishing Treasures Resources

Vanishing Treasures Resources are defined as a structure or grouping of related structures that:

- Are in a "ruined" state.
- Have exposed intact fabric (earthen, stone, wood, etc.).
- Are not being used for their original function.
- Occupation and utilization have been interrupted or discontinued for an extended period of time.
- Are located in the arid west.
- Are the resources or part of the resources for which the park was created, or, National Historic Landmark, listed on, or eligible for listing on the National Register of Historic Places?

Examples of Vanishing Treasures Resources:

- Architectural remains that have intact historic fabric exposed at or above grade, including: wall alignments, upright slabs, foundations, bins, cists, constructed hearths.
- Sub-grade architecture exposed through excavation or erosion (i.e., pithouses, dugouts, cists, etc.).
- Native American architectural structures (i.e., pueblos, cliff dwellings, hogans, wickiups, ramadas, corrals, earthen architecture, etc.).
- EuroAmerican architectural structures (i.e., churches, convents, forts, ranch-farm structures/homesteads, mine buildings, acequias or related features, kilns, etc.).
-

Examples of Non-Vanishing Treasures Resources:

- Sites with no exposed architecture or structural remains, (i.e., collapsed, buried, mounded, or otherwise not evident).
- Archeological or other sites with no architectural remains (i.e., lithic scatters, dumps, campsites, etc).
- Civilian Conservation Corp (CCC) and Civil Works Administration (CWA) buildings and features.
- Historic structures which are regularly maintained, and/or adaptively used, and fit within the Historic Structures/List of Classified Structures (LCS) definitions.
- Structures in use as National Park Service facilities (i.e., administrative buildings, trails, bridges, ditches, canals, etc).

- Mine shafts, caves, which do not have architectural/structural features.
- Pictographs, petroglyphs, rock art, etc., except if found in or on architectural structures.
- National Park Service or other reconstructed buildings or ruins (i.e., Aztec Great Kiva, Bents Old Fort).

Note: It is acknowledged that often times the traditionally associated communities to whom many of the involved Vanishing Treasures resources/archeological sites hold importance, do not consider them to be unoccupied, out of use, or abandoned. "Ruins" are considered by some groups to be spiritually inhabited and are considered to be "in use" by virtue of being invoked in prayers, songs, stories, etc. They are considered dynamic parts of active cultural systems. While we use the term "ruins" and the associated definition, it is recognize that some communities do not use the term "ruin" nor consider the places to be

Ruins Preservation Terminology

Condition

Good
The site shows no clear evidence of major negative disturbance and deterioration by natural and/or human forces. The site's archeological values remain well preserved, and no site treatment actions required in the near future to maintain its condition.

Fair
The site shows clear evidence of minor disturbance and deterioration by natural and/or human forces, and some degree of corrective action should be carried out fairly soon to protect the site.

Poor
The site shows clear evidence of major disturbance and rapid deterioration by natural and/or human forces, and immediate corrective action is required to protect and preserve the site.

Intensity of On-Site Erosion

Severe
The site will be significantly damaged or lost if action is not taken immediately.

Moderate
For an impact to be considered moderate, it must meet at least one of the following criteria: The site will be significantly damaged or lost if action is not taken in the immediate future. The site has been damaged and some integrity has been lost.

Low
The continuing effect of the impact is known but it will not result in significant or irreparable damage to the site.

None
The site has not been obviously impacted.

Integrity

Integrity refers to how much of the structure remains standing and intact. For example, a structure that only has one complete wall standing and intact would be given a value of 20%. A structure with all four walls standing and intact, plus an intact roof and floor, would be given a value of 100%.

Stability

Stability refers to a wall or structure's state of equilibrium.

Stable
A structure that maintains consistency of composition and components with little or no sign of erosion that would lead to any form of structural degradation.

The term stable can also be applied to structures that have essentially deteriorated to grade and thus have little or no standing structural remains above the ground surface that would be subject to further deterioration.

Partially Stable
A structure that exhibits signs of whole or partial degradation of the existing composition and components such that structural stability is threatened.

Unstable
A structure that has suffered damage from erosive forces such that structural collapse or complete degradation is imminent.

Project Funding for 2006

PARK	PMIS NUMBER	FY 2006 PROGRAM STATUS VANISHING TREASURES PROGRAM - FUND 01	PMIS ALLOCATION	ADJUSTMENT INC/DEC
		PROGRAM PROJECTED ALLOCATION	$ 1,090,700	
		Authorized amount has changed $11,200	$ 11,200	
			$ 1,101,900	
IMRO	no number	VT Program Management	$20,000	
IMRO	no number	VT Leadership/Advisory Group Coordination	$20,000	
IMRO	no number	VT Support Staff	$20,000	
ZION	107322	Document and Prepare Treatment Strategy for Sites in Parunweap Canyon	$64,600	
SOAR	107468A	Preservation Treatment and Documentation of Lime Kilns at SAGU	$86,100	
ZION	107293A	Architectural Documentation of Four Historic Irrigation Ditches in Zion Canyon	$54,300	
WUPA	96619B	Perform Emergency Treatment/Repairs for Kaibab House Pueblo	$113,100	
CHCU	106627A	Develop Backfill/Drainage Plan for Pueblo Bonito and Implement Initial Treatment Phase	$98,000	
TONT	107603A	(Phase II) Implement Preservation Treatments at Three Primary Cliff Dwellings (TONT85A-39, 44, 50)	$120,300	
PECO	87434A	CULTURAL CYCLIC (&VT): Repair and Stabilize Adobe Spanish Structures	$49,000	
GRCA	108041A	Dating, Architectural Documentation, and Stabilization of Historic Wickiups and Sweatlodges	$59,200	
GLCA	116047A	Assess Condition and Perform Cyclic Maintenance at Seven Sites in Glen Canyon (VT)	$58,100	Projects will be entered PARK$
CANY	114802A	Complete River Corridor Vanishing Treasures Condition Assessment	$106,100	
WUPA/WACA	107254	Formal Condition Assessment of Third Fort, Walnut Canyon	$111,200	
MOJA	103287A	Condition Assessment/Treatment Plan for Historic Evening Star Mine Headframe and Related Structures	$50,000	
BAND	114548A	Emergency Conservation of Frjoles Canyon Cavates FY06	$71,600	Requested $124,800
		ALLOCATED	$ 1,101,600	
		LEFT TO ALLOCATE	$ 300	
		TOTAL	$ 1,101,600	

Table 4.1.

Funding Comparisons

Table 5.1. Personnel Funding 2005 (In Thousands of Dollars)

	Arizona	California	Colorado	New Mexico	Texas	Utah	Wyoming	Program Total by FY
FY 1998	269	0	67	117	0	0	0	453
FY 1999	240	0	4	547	71	0	0	862
FY 2000	256	0	261	113	165	0	0	1,315
FY 2001	68	0	0	168	0	0	0	236
FY 2002	58	0	0	126	0	251	0	435
FY 2003	327	0	0	126	72	75	0	671
FY 2004	143	0	162	0	70	0	0	375
FY 2005	249	0	0	107	0	95	0	451
State Total	1,361	0	494	1,197	378	326	0	*4,798*

Table 5.2. Project Funding 2005 (In Thousands of Dollars)

	Arizona	California	Colorado	New Mexico	Texas	Utah	Wyoming	Program Total by FY
FY 1998	272	0	67	213.3	0	0	0	552.3
FY 1999	166	0	4	198.5	10	65	0	443.5
FY 2000	345	0	261	235	0	125	0	966
FY 2001	849	0	0	275.7	104	145	0	1,373.7
FY 2002	386	0	0	347.3	88	80.4	0	901.7
FY 2003	312	0	0	428	0	0	0	740
FY 2004	382	0	162	356.8	0	95.3	0	996.1
FY 2005	391	0	124	371.7	44	129.4	0	1,060.1
State Total	3,103	0	618	2,426.3	246	640.1	0	*7,033.4*

Vanishing Treasures Sustainable Pest Management Workshop, March 2006

Casa Grande Site Visit
2005 Vanishing Treasures Leadership Committee

Joshua Tree

Death Valley

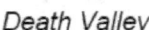

Manzanar

Vanishing

Arizona

1. Canyon De Chelly National Monument
2. Casa Grande Ruins National Monument
3. Coronado National Memorial
4. Fort Bowie National Historic Site
5. Grand Canyon National Park
6. Montezuma Castle National Monument
7. Navajo National Monument
8. Organ Pipe Cactus National Monument
9. Petrified Forest National Park
10. Saguaro National Park
11. Tonto National Monument
12. Tumacacori National Historical Park
13. Tuzigoot National Monument
14. Walnut Canyon National Monument
15. Wupatki National Monument

California / Nevada

16. Death Valley National Park
17. Joshua Tree National Park
18. Mojave National Preserve
19. Manzanar National Historic Site

Colorado

20. Colorado National Monument
21. Dinosaur National Monument (Also Utah)
22. Mesa Verde National Park

New Mexico

23. Aztec Ruins National Monument
24. Bandelier National Monument
25. Chaco Culture National Historical Park
26. El Malpais National Monument
27. El Morro National Monument
28. Fort Union National Monument
29. Gila Cliff Dwellings National Monument
30. Pecos National Historical Park
31. Salinas Pueblo Missions National Monument

Texas

32. Big Bend National Park
33. Fort Davis National Historic Site
34. Guadalupe Mountains National Park
35. Lake Meredith National Recreation Area
36. San Antonio Missions National Historical Park

Utah

37. Arches National Park
38. Capital Reef National Park
39. Canyonlands National Park
40. Glen Canyon National Recreation Area
   (Also Arizona)
41. Golden Spike National Historic Site
42. Hovenweep National Monument
   (Also Colorado)
43. Natural Bridges National Monument
44. Zion National Park

Wyoming

45. Fort Laramie National Historic Site

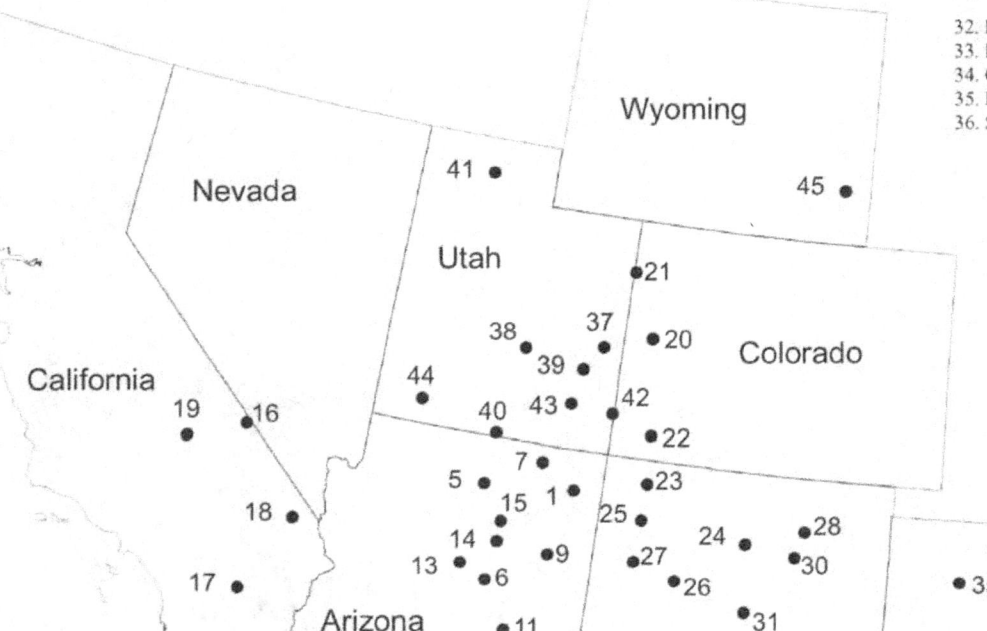

Vanishing Treasures Parks

National Park Service
U.S. Department of the Interior

Vanishing Treasures, 2006